RICH LANDS AND POOR

The Road to World Prosperity

WORLD PERSPECTIVES

Volumes already published

WORLD PERSPECTIVES • *Volume Sixteen*

Planned and Edited by RUTH NANDA ANSHEN

RICH LANDS AND POOR
The Road to World Prosperity

BY GUNNAR MYRDAL

New York

HARPER & BROTHERS PUBLISHERS

Contents

PART ONE

THE MECHANISM OF NATIONAL AND INTER-
NATIONAL ECONOMIC INEQUALITY

PART TWO

ECONOMIC INEQUALITIES, THE PUBLIC
CONSCIENCE AND ECONOMIC THEORY

World Perspectives
What This Series Means

⌈IT IS the thesis of *World Perspectives* that man is in the process of
developing a new consciousness which, in spite of his apparent
spiritual and moral captivity, can eventually lift the human race
above and beyond the fear, ignorance, and isolation which beset it
today.⌋ It is to this nascent consciousness, to this concept of man born
out of a universe perceived through a fresh vision of reality, that
World Perspectives is dedicated.

Only those spiritual and intellectual leaders of our epoch who
have a paternity in this extension of man's horizons are invited to
participate in this Series: those who are aware of the truth that
beyond the divisiveness among men there exists a primordial unitive
power since we are all bound together by a common humanity more
fundamental than any unity of dogma; those who recognize that the
centrifugal force which has scattered and atomized mankind must be
replaced by an integrating structure and process capable of bestow-
ing meaning and purpose on existence; those who realize that science
itself, when not inhibited by the limitations of its own methodology,
when chastened and humbled, commits man to an indeterminate
range of yet undreamed consequences that may flow from it.

This Series endeavors to point to a reality of which scientific
theory has revealed only one aspect. It is the commitment to this
reality that lends universal intent to a scientist's most original and
solitary thought. By acknowledging this frankly we shall restore
science to the great family of human aspirations by which men hope
to fulfill themselves in the world community as thinking and sentient
beings. For our problem is to discover a principle of differentiation
and yet relationship lucid enough to justify and to purify scientific,
philosophic and all other knowledge, both discursive and intuitive,

by accepting their interdependence. This is the crisis in consciousness made articulate through the crisis in science. This is the new awakening.

Each volume presents the thought and belief of its author and points to the way in which religion, philosophy, art, science, economics, politics and history may constitute that form of human activity which takes the fullest and most precise account of variousness, possibility, complexity and difficulty. Thus *World Perspectives* endeavors to define that ecumenical power of the mind and heart which enables man through his mysterious greatness to re-create his life.

This Series is committed to a re-examination of all those sides of human endeavor which the specialist was taught to believe he could safely leave aside. It interprets present and past events impinging on human life in our growing World Age and envisages what man may yet attain when summoned by an unbending inner necessity to the quest of what is most exalted in him. Its purpose is to offer new vistas in terms of world and human development while refusing to betray the intimate correlation between universality and individuality, dynamics and form, freedom and destiny. Each author deals with the increasing realization that spirit and nature are not separate and apart; that intuition and reason must regain their importance as the means of perceiving and fusing inner being with outer reality.

World Perspectives endeavors to show that the doctrine of wholeness, unity, organism is a higher and more concrete conception than that of matter and energy. Thus an enlarged meaning of life, of biology, not as it is revealed in the test tube of the laboratory but as it is experienced within the organism of life itself, is attempted in this Series. For the principle of life consists in the tension which connects spirit with the realm of matter. The element of life is dominant in the very texture of nature, thus rendering life, biology, a transempirical science. The laws of life have their origin beyond their mere physical manifestations and compel us to consider their spiritual source. In fact, the widening of the conceptual framework has not only served to restore order within the respective branches of knowledge, but has also disclosed analogies in man's position regarding the analysis and synthesis of experience in apparently separated domains of knowledge suggesting the possibility of an ever more embracing objective description of the meaning of life.

Knowledge, it is shown in these books, no longer consists in a manipulation of man and nature as opposite forces, nor in the reduction of data to mere statistical order, but is a means of liberating mankind from the destructive power of fear, pointing the way toward the goal of the rehabilitation of the human will and the rebirth of faith and confidence in the human person. The works published also endeavor to reveal that the cry for patterns, systems and authorities is growing less insistent as the desire grows stronger in both East and West for the recovery of a dignity, integrity and self-realization which are the inalienable rights of man who may now guide change by means of conscious purpose in the light of rational experience.

Other vital questions explored relate to problems of international understanding as well as to problems dealing with prejudice and the resultant tensions and antagonisms. The growing perception and responsibility of our World Age point to the new reality that the individual person and the collective person supplement and integrate each other; that the thrall of totalitarianism of both left and right has been shaken in the universal desire to recapture the authority of truth and human totality. Mankind can finally place its trust not in a proletarian authoritarianism, not in a secularized humanism, both of which have betrayed the spiritual property right of history, but in a sacramental brotherhood and in the unity of knowledge. This new consciousness has created a widening of human horizons beyond every parochialism, and a revolution in human thought comparable to the basic assumption, among the ancient Greeks, of the sovereignty of reason; corresponding to the great effulgence of the moral conscience articulated by the Hebrew prophets; analogous to the fundamental assertions of Christianity; or to the beginning of a new scientific era, the era of the science of dynamics, the experimental foundations of which were laid by Galileo in the Renaissance.

An important effort of this Series is to re-examine the contradictory meanings and applications which are given today to such terms as democracy, freedom, justice, love, peace, brotherhood and

God. The purpose of such inquiries is to clear the way for the foundation of a genuine *world* history not in terms of nation or race or culture but in terms of man in relation to God, to himself, his fellow man and the universe, that reach beyond immediate self-interest. For the meaning of the World Age consists in respecting man's hopes and dreams which lead to a deeper understanding of the basic values of all peoples.

World Perspectives is planned to gain insight into the meaning of man, who not only is determined by history but who also determines history. History is to be understood as concerned not only with the life of man on this planet but as including also such cosmic influences as interpenetrate our human world. This generation is discovering that history does not conform to the social optimism of modern civilization and that the organization of human communities and the establishment of freedom and peace are not only intellectual achievements but spiritual and moral achievements as well, demanding a cherishing of the wholeness of human personality, the "unmediated wholeness of feeling and thought," and constituting a never-ending challenge to man, emerging from the abyss of meaninglessness and suffering, to be renewed and replenished in the totality of his life.

Justice itself, which has been "in a state of pilgrimage and crucifixion" and now is being slowly liberated from the grip of social and political demonologies in the East as well as in the West, begins to question its own premises. The modern revolutionary movements which have challenged the sacred institutions of society by protecting social injustice in the name of social justice are examined and re-evaluated.

In the light of this, we have no choice but to admit that the *un*-freedom against which freedom is measured must be retained with it, namely, that the aspect of truth out of which the night view appears to emerge, the darkness of our time, is as little abandonable as is man's subjective advance. Thus the two sources of man's consciousness are inseparable, not as dead but as living and complementary, an aspect of that "principle of complementarity" through which Niels Bohr has sought to unite the quantum and the wave. This unity is the very fabric of life's radiant energy.

There is in mankind today a counterforce to the sterility and danger of a quantitative, anonymous mass culture, a new, if sometimes imperceptible, spiritual sense of convergence toward world unity on the basis of the sacredness of each human person and respect for the plurality of cultures. There is a growing awareness that equality may not be evaluated in mere numerical terms but is proportionate and analogical in its reality. For when equality is equated with interchangeability, individuality is negated and the human person extinguished.

We stand at the brink of an age of a world in which human life presses forward to actualize new forms. The false separation of man and nature, of time and space, of freedom and security, is acknowledged and we are faced with a new vision of man in his organic unity and of history offering a richness and diversity of quality and majesty of scope hitherto unprecedented. In relating the accumulated wisdom of man's spirit to the new reality of the World Age, in articulating its thought and belief, *World Perspectives* seeks to encourage a renaissance of hope in society and of pride in man's decision as to what his destiny will be.

World Perspectives is committed to the recognition that all great changes are preceded by a vigorous intellectual reevaluation and reorganization. Our authors are aware that the sin of *hubris* may be avoided by showing that the creative process itself is not a free activity if by free we mean arbitrary, or unrelated to cosmic law. For the creative process in the human mind, the developmental processes in organic nature and the basic laws of the inorganic realm may be but varied expressions of a universal formative process. Thus *World Perspectives* hopes to show that although the present apocalyptic period is one of exceptional tensions, there is also at work an exceptional movement toward a compensating unity which refuses to violate the ultimate moral power at work in the universe, that very power upon which all human effort must at last depend. In this way we may come to understand that there exists an inherent independence of spiritual and mental growth which though conditioned by circumstances is never determined by circumstances. In this way the great plethora of human knowledge may be correlated with an insight into the nature of human nature by being attuned to the wide and deep range of human thought and human experience.

In spite of the infinite obligation of men and in spite of their finite power, in spite of the intransigence of nationalisms, and in spite of the homelessness of moral passions rendered ineffectual by the scientific outlook, beneath the apparent turmoil and upheaval of the present, and out of the transformations of this dynamic period with the unfolding of a world consciousness, the purpose of *World Perspectives* is to help quicken the "unshaken heart of well-rounded truth" and interpret the significant elements of the World Age now taking shape out of the core of that undimmed continuity of the creative process which restores man to mankind while deepening and enhancing his communion with the universe.

RUTH NANDA ANSHEN

New York, 1958

Preface

IN OCTOBER, 1955, at the invitation of the National Bank of Egypt, I gave the Anniversary Commemoration Lectures in Cairo. The lectures were later published by the bank under the title: *Development and Underdevelopment: A Note on the Mechanism of National and International Economic Inequality* (Cairo, 1956). I am grateful to the bank for doing me the honor of inviting me as guest lecturer, for publishing my lectures, and for now permitting me to reissue them in a revised version.

In preparing the text for the present volume I have made the revision as thorough as I could without increasing too much the length of the manuscript. From the original lectures I have permitted myself to preserve, however, both the nontechnical treatment of problems and the informal and sometimes personal manner of expression.

About the contents I can be brief. I take it for granted that the rapid growth of writings on the economic problems of underdeveloped countries reflects the fundamental change in the international political situation since the Second World War. In selecting as topic for my lectures the subject I have mentioned I was aware that I was merely following in the general stream of this adjustment of the social sciences to the new political situation in the world.

The complex of problems facing underdeveloped countries can, however, be viewed from many angles: different questions can be asked and different approaches chosen. It is, indeed, in the interest of a balanced growth of scientific knowledge that many individual students should simultaneously tackle problems in many different ways. In the great humanistic tradition of rationalism, our faith is that in the field of social sciences as in other fields of endeavor progress will come as the result of discussion and even of controversy.

I have here chosen to focus attention on one particular aspect of the international situation, namely, the very large and steadily increasing economic inequalities between developed and underdeveloped countries. Though these inequalities and their tendency to grow are flagrant realities, and though they form a basic cause of the international tension in our present world, they are usually not treated as a central problem in the literature on underdevelopment and development.

This is, however, precisely what I want to do. My purpose is to inquire why and how these inequalities came to exist, why they persist, and why they tend to increase. In Chapter VII I shall also touch on another question: how could these trends be reversed? A rational answer to this last question—which concerns policy and where the reasoning proceeds in terms of means and ends rather than causes and effects—will have to be based upon knowledge of the causal mechanism by which the inequalities came to exist.

Part II, on Economic Inequality, the Public Conscience and Economic Theory, corresponds to the first lecture in the series as originally delivered. In its present form this part of the text was written to serve as a critical introduction to the book. When finally preparing the manuscript for printing, I decided, however, to transfer these chapters to their present position. The reader who is not particularly interested in the philosophical basis, and the inherited predilections, of our thinking on economic problems should, I felt, have the right to get immediately to the substance of what positively I have to say on the main question I have raised.

I felt also that there is a possibility that some readers who will not agree with my opinions in the critical part may better tackle the positive part of the argument, if their feelings have not been hurt in advance by having read the critical part. Indeed, I felt a hope that the content of the positive part might even bring them to a better understanding of why I have so consistently preserved a critical attitude toward certain elements in our inherited economic theory.

But, independently of the order of presenting the thoughts, this remains an economist's book on his attitude toward economic theory. As this attitude of the author has a long history from his first scientific endeavors, the reader will have to excuse references back to his earlier writings. The argument moves on a general and methodological plane in the sense that the theory is discussed as a complex of broad structures of thought. I bring in specific facts only when necessary for stating problems or as checks on the applicability of theory in explaining reality; and figures are left out altogether.

The value premises which determine my viewpoint are the desirability of political democracy and of equality of opportunity. For an explanation of the great importance which I attach to the principle of working with explicit value premises and for a more precise definition of those actually used in these lectures I refer the reader to my book, *An International Economy* (Harper, New York, 1956)—in particular to the Preface, Chapter II, the Appendix—and to those of my earlier publications cited in footnote 1 to that Appendix.

Though the argument is presented in a general form, my purpose is to help to make theory more realistic. In the larger book I just mentioned, and to which these lectures are complementary, I have attempted a more detailed and concrete treatment of the problems of economic underdevelopment and development but I have there referred only in passing to the present issue of the mechanism of equality and inequality.

The exposition refers exclusively to the non-Soviet world. In the Soviet orbit a different economic system is in force: within the single countries there is not only central state planning but also public ownership of the means of production; international economic relations are determined by state monopoly.

I do not want to exaggerate the relevance for economic analysis of this distinction between the two economic systems. I believe that the principle of circular and cumulative causation would have its application in the Soviet world, too, in explaining development trends as well as in determining policy. And I would personally be greatly interested in pursuing my study into the realm of Soviet economy.

Moreover, I hold that there is no rational ground for assuming as immutable the sharp division of the world economy into "the two parallel world markets" which Stalin proclaimed and which he was so largely responsible for having created, implying among other things a remarkable lack of diversification of state policy within the Soviet orbit. World development during the past half century should have made us aware that nothing is permanent—particularly not the political development in various countries and their arrangement in different camps according to ideologies—and that the only certainty is that we shall continuously be surprised by seeing the unexpected happen.

But as a practical device, and in order to keep the line of reasoning simple and clear in this brief presentation, which is so much in the nature of an abstract outline, I have preferred to restrict my range of vision to the non-Soviet world.

G. M.

Geneva
August 1, 1957

Part One

The Mechanism of National and
International Economic Inequality

I.

An Unexplained General Trait of Social Reality

International Economic Inequalities

THE FACTS of international economic inequalities in the present world, when viewed in the very broadest perspective, fall into a definite and simple pattern.[1]

A few countries are highly developed economically and have very high levels of average real income per head. Richest of all are those of the former British colonies which are located in the temperate zones and became populated mainly by European stock, i.e., the United States and Canada, Australia and New Zealand. The countries in northwestern and west central Europe also belong to this group. Together the inhabitants of these few countries make up about one-sixth of the total population in the non-Soviet world.

This is the economic upper class of nations in world society. The lower class of nations is far bigger: more than two-thirds of the people in the non-Soviet world live in countries where real income per head is only a very tiny fraction of what it is in the highly developed countries and, indeed, in most cases is much smaller than it was in those countries before they started to develop rapidly a century or more ago.[2]

[1] For verification of the broad survey of international economic inequalities in this section, I refer to the latest publications of the United Nations and the Secretariats of the three regional Economic Commissions.

[2] Cf. also Simon Kuznets, "Underdeveloped Countries and the Pre-

To this majority group of very poor nations belong all the peoples of Africa except the white settlers in South Africa, entrenched behind their Apartheid legislation, and similar, though smaller, enclaves of white people in other parts of that continent which is still largely carved up into colonial possessions of West European powers. The whole of non-Soviet Asia belongs to this group of very poor countries, including the countries in the Middle and Near East. Finally, it includes the larger part of Latin America, which has, however, a few countries which have reached a "middle-class" position, like Argentina or Uruguay.

In the highly developed countries all indices point steadily upward. On the average and in the longer span there are no signs of a slackening of the momentum of economic development in those countries. Looking backward, business slumps and big depressions and even severe setbacks due to wars appear only as short-term waverings of the firmly rising long-term trend. In the period after the Second World War these countries have seen their labor and other productive resources constantly in work at full capacity. The general expectancy in these countries of a continued rapid economic development is part of the commonly shared assumptions on the basis of which national life evolves toward ever higher realization of democracy and national integration.

It is on the whole the industrialized countries which are industrializing further. By far the greater portion of the non-Soviet world's total savings originates in this smaller part of it where incomes are high. As new inventions are constantly raising the demand for capital, almost all of the available capital is invested there. If one counted as home investment also the expenditure made for building up the closely controlled enclaves for exploiting oil and mineral resources in the poorer countries, this would appear to be the case even more completely.

In the underdeveloped countries, on the other hand, where incomes are so very much lower, capital formation and investment tend generally to be smaller, even relative to their lower incomes. For

industrial Phase in the Advanced Countries: An Attempt at Comparison." Paper to the *World Population Conference,* Rome, 1954 (to be published).

equality in rate of development, they would instead need to be relatively bigger, as in the poorer countries the natural population increase is usually faster. The faster population increase is a result of a particular relation between fertility and mortality rates, where both are on a very high level, which, in addition, tends to make the age distribution of their populations relatively less advantageous. As a consequence of all this—and of the tradition of stagnation which has entrenched itself in their entire culture—their economic development usually proceeds more slowly. Many of these countries have during recent decades even moved backward in average income.

Levels of income per head differ greatly among these very poor countries. In South and East Asia the differences are quite big even between neighboring countries and the same is true in the other major regions where underdeveloped countries are found.

And everywhere in the underdeveloped part of the world there are countries or regions of countries which are experiencing rapid economic development. Even in Africa there are areas with feverish investment and mounting production, always connected with outside economic exploitation of their natural resources.

In the Middle East the general poverty is so great that the Palestine refugees, herded together in pitiful quarters in camps—which they themselves prevent from being improved in order not to prejudice their claims to return to Palestine—and mainly supported on the United Nations' grant of annually about $40 per head, are estimated to enjoy a higher standard of living than broad masses of poor Arabs in the surrounding countries, and sometimes higher than they themselves once enjoyed in Palestine before their eviction.

But in the eastern part of the region the oil-producing countries—or rather their rulers—draw royalties and other oil revenues which are said now to amount to one billion dollars a year; in ten years' time they are expected to increase to three billion dollars a year. On the Mediterranean coast the tiny Israel, not endowed with a very bountiful nature and under constant threat of being overwhelmed by the rising flood of the hostile Arab nations surrounding it but being financially supported by world Jewry, is developing very rapidly under great stress and strain. In Lebanon, Beirut is an old and rich trading center.

In Latin America many countries, even besides those cited above as having reached a middle-class position, have experienced a considerable economic development in recent decades, though it has been unstable in time and uneven. On the whole it has been limited to the ports and cities and has left the rural masses in stagnation and destitution.

The great differences between countries within both groups in actual economic levels, as well as in current development rates and development rates during different periods in the near past, do not invalidate the following broad generalizations:

> That there is a small group of countries which are quite well off and a much larger group of extremely poor countries;
>
> that the countries in the former group are on the whole firmly settled in a pattern of continuing economic development, while in the latter group average progress is slower, as many countries are in constant danger of not being able to lift themselves out of stagnation or even of losing ground so far as average income levels are concerned; and
>
> that, therefore, on the whole, in recent decades the economic inequalities between developed and underdeveloped countries have been increasing.

This trend toward international economic inequality stands out in contrast to what is happening within the rich countries individually. There the trend has, in recent generations, been toward greater equality of opportunity, and this development has been an accelerating one which is still gaining momentum. The contrary development for the world as a whole should be related also to the fact that as yet there has been no real parallel within the poorer countries individually to the equalization process now going on in the rich countries. Most of the poorer countries have preserved as great internal inequalities among individuals, classes and regions as there have ever been; in many of them the inequalities are still growing.

In the highly developed countries there has been spectacular progress of which we, who live there, are acutely conscious. The poorer, underdeveloped countries, which on the average are developing more slowly, form, however, much the larger part of the world; again on the average, the population growth has been more rapid there than in the small group of rich countries. With these two facts in mind, it becomes very uncertain whether and in what sense it can be held that there has in recent decades been any economic progress at all for mankind as a whole.

Increasing Awareness

Other facts basic to our problem are the political ones:

The peoples in the underdeveloped countries are becoming increasingly aware of these huge international inequalities and the danger that they will continue to grow; and these peoples and their spokesmen show an inclination to put part of the blame for their poverty on the rest of the world and, in particular, on the countries which are better off—or, rather, they see a cause of the inequalities in the world economic system which keeps them so poor while other nations are so rich and becoming richer.

The Second World War helped to release many checks and controls upholding the established power system in the world, and one of its results was the liberation on a vast scale of subject peoples from colonial rule. A very important characteristic of the new nationalism which was born in this process is, however, that the demand of the peoples is for equality of opportunity with other peoples as well as for liberty. All these very poor nations, as they are touched by the Great Awakening, crave economic development as well as national independence.

It is interesting to note in this connection that now we have all come to refer to this majority of very poor countries as "the underdeveloped countries." This dynamic term, which gained its present prevalence only after the Second World War, itself indicates the great change in the world political situation to which I have referred. The expression commonly used until quite recently was the static term "the backward countries."

Both terms—like all the fundamental concepts of the social sciences—are value-loaded,[3] and it is conducive to clarity in our thinking that we are aware of this fact. The use of the concept "the underdeveloped countries" implies the value judgment that it is an accepted goal of public policy that the countries so designated should experience economic development. It is with this implication that people in the poorer countries use the term and press its usage upon people in the richer countries. When they, in their turn, accept this term and suppress the old one, "the backward countries," they also accept the implication.

The change from the static to the dynamic concept thus implies in the richer countries a registration of a positive attitude to the Great Awakening in the poorer countries and, therefore, an acknowledgment—given, naturally, only in a general and therefore necessarily vague form—that those countries are right in demanding higher standards of income, a bigger share in the good things of life, and greater equality of opportunity.

As part of the same intellectual realignment, the broad facts of international economic inequalities, referred to above, have begun to be disseminated ever more widely, not only in the underdeveloped countries, where they furnish part of the driving force in the political process I refer to as the Great Awakening, but also in the developed ones.

It can be seen that when ordinary people in our developed countries are for the first time made aware of these stern facts, this experience often has the character of a revelation to them; it can also be observed that the new knowledge is felt to be awkward. Their general concept of the world, as it is and as it ought to be, cannot easily be adjusted to a realization of all this abject poverty in most of the world and of the tendency for international inequalities to grow.

The discussion of the reaction of the public conscience to the facts of economic inequalities is pursued further in Part II of this volume.

The Inadequacy of the Inherited Theoretical Approach

In Part II, which, as I explained in the Preface, is nothing else

[3] This is not meant in a critical sense; see *An International Economy*, Appendix. "Methodological Note on the Concepts and the Value Premises," pp. 336 ff., and earlier writings cited in footnote 1 to the Appendix, p. 365.

than a displaced introduction, I also discuss the very apparent inadequacy of our inherited theoretical approach to come to grips with
the problem of the economic inequalities. More specifically, I point
out that a study, however intensive, of the theory of international
trade cannot provide much of an explanation in causal terms of how
the facts of international economic inequalities have come into existence and why there is a tendency for the inequalities to grow. The
theory of international trade and, indeed, economic theory generally
were never worked out to serve the purpose of explaining the reality
of economic underdevelopment and development.

To understand why economic theory has developed in this way
requires an immanent criticism of its inherited predilections. This is
attempted in Part II. On the more superficial level of mere logic,
the explanation is the unrealistic assumptions for theory.

Stable equilibrium is one such unrealistic assumption. In its un-
complicated form it implies the notions that every disturbance pro-
vokes a reaction within the system, directed toward restoring a new
state of equilibrium, and that action and reaction will meet in one
and the same time space. An economic system which is not in rest is
for this reason always moving toward equilibrium, though not necessarily the straight way. It is usually also conceded that every new
primary change and, in addition, the fact that continuously the
system is not resting in equilibrium will change the virtual equilibrium position toward which it is moving. Implied in the stable
equilibrium notion and preserved even in its most relativistic forms
is the idea that, when a change calls forth other changes as reaction,
these secondary changes are counterdirected to the primary change.

To the credit of this assumption can be counted that it represents
an easily available theoretical means to comprehend and demonstrate in a simple manner the universal interdependence between all
the factors in the economic system. It constitutes also an almost
indispensable logical step in many economic arguments.

In our tradition the stable equilibrium assumption has become
something of a general thought-form: indeed, the essence of the
approach which is associated with the idea of a single and central
economic theory. Few economists even among those who have

criticized the notion of stable equilibrium will altogether escape its influence on their thinking. As I point out in Chapter X, it is imbued with a teleological intent and is related to powerful predilections, all rooted firmly in the traditions of economic theory from its early origin and in the philosophies which were, and continuously are, this theory's logical basis.

The notion that there are certain elements of social reality which can be characterized as "the economic factors" and that a theoretical analysis can be rationally restricted to the interactions of those factors constitutes another unrealistic assumption. It is closely related to the equilibrium assumption. For it is precisely in the realm of that large part of social reality which is left outside the economic analysis by the abstraction from "the noneconomic factors" that the equilibrium assumption falls to the ground. Those noneconomic factors cannot be taken for given and static; when they react, they normally do so in a disequilibrating way.

In reality, there is, of course, no distinction between facts corresponding to our traditional scholastic divisions of social science into separate disciplines. A realistic analysis of problems can never stop at such lines of division. The distinction between factors that are "economic" and those that are "noneconomic" is, indeed, a useless and nonsensical device from the point of view of logic, and should be replaced by a distinction between "relevant" and "irrelevant" factors or "more relevant" and "less relevant." And this latter dividing line should not be expected to be the same for different problems.

The international inequalities are, of course, not dissimilar from the regional inequalities within a country. We will also find that there is a very close causal interrelation between the two. For these reasons I shall devote two chapters—III and IV—to the regional inequalities within a country.

II.

The Principle of Circular and Cumulative Causation

The Vague Notion of the Vicious Circle

ALMOST all students of problems connected with underdevelopment and development will be found, in one connection or another, to have made a reference to the "vicious circle." Professor C. E. A. Winslow, for instance, in a book devoted to the economics of health, points out: "It was clear . . . that poverty and disease formed a vicious circle. Men and women were sick because they were poor; they became poorer because they were sick, and sicker because they were poorer." [1] Winslow thus points to a circular and cumulative process, continuously pressing levels downward, in which one negative factor is, at the same time, both cause and effect of other negative factors.

In the same spirit, Professor Ragnar Nurkse, when giving the 1952 Commemoration Lectures in Cairo, referred to the "vicious circle of poverty" and explained:

The concept implies, of course, a circular constellation of forces tending to act and react upon one another in such a way as to keep a poor country in a state of poverty. Particular instances of such circular constellations are not difficult to im-

[1] C. E. A. Winslow, *The Cost of Sickness and the Price of Health*, Monograph Series, No. 7, Geneva, 1951, p. 9; also Gunnar Myrdal, "Economic Aspects of Health," Chron. World Health Organisation, Geneva, 1952, 6, No. 7–8.

agine. For example, a poor man may not have enough to eat; being under-nourished, his health may be weak; being physically weak, his working capacity may be low, which means that he is poor, which in turn means that he will not have enough to eat; and so on. A situation of this sort, applying to a country as a whole, can be summed up in the trite proposition: "a country is poor because it is poor." [2]

Quite obviously a circular relationship between less poverty, more food, improved health and higher working capacity would sustain a cumulative process upward instead of downward.

The whole American folklore built around the tendency for people to want to jump on the bandwagon is centered around a conception of an upward spiral. So is, of course, also the expression in America which is so typical of their optimistic go-getting culture: "Nothing succeeds like success." To this, which is by itself so eminently true, must be added, in order to preserve the balance, a reminder of the truth also of the traditional idea of the "vicious circle" downward: Nothing fails like failure.

As so very often is the case, the Bible gives a perfect expression of this ancient folk wisdom: "For unto every one that hath shall be given, and he shall have abundance: but from him that hath not shall be taken away even that which he hath." [3] In this admirable statement the truth is seen that the cumulative process goes in both directions. And there is voiced also an understanding of the fact, which in our analysis will be given much importance, namely, that the cumulative process, if not regulated, will cause increasing inequalities.

Stable Equilibrium a False Analogy

In this volume I shall attempt to give a more definite formulation

[2] Ragnar Nurkse, *Some Aspects of Capital Accumulation in Underdeveloped Countries,* Cairo, 1952; cf. Ragnar Nurkse, *Problems of Capital Formation in Underdeveloped Countries,* Oxford, 1953, pp. 4 f.

[3] Matthew 25:29; cf. 13:12. Cf. the folksy American expression: "Them as has gits." A peasant in southern Portugal was heard saying: "Those who have something here, get everything, but those who have not anything, get nothing."

to this vague idea of the circular causation of a cumulative process. It is my conviction that this idea contains *in nuce* the approach to a more realistic analysis of social change—indeed a vision of the general theory of underdevelopment and development which we are all yearning for.

Expressed first in negative terms, my starting point is the assertion that the notion of stable equilibrium is normally a false analogy to choose when constructing a theory to explain the changes in a social system. What is wrong with the stable equilibrium assumption as applied to social reality is the very idea that a social process follows a direction—though it might move toward it in a circuitous way— toward a position which in some sense or other can be described as a state of equilibrium between forces. Behind this idea is another and still more basic assumption, namely, that a change will regularly call forth a reaction in the system in the form of changes which on the whole go in the contrary direction to the first change.

The idea I want to expound in this book is that, on the contrary, in the normal case there is no such tendency toward automatic self-stabilization in the social system. The system is by itself not moving toward any sort of balance between forces but is constantly on the move away from such a situation. In the normal case a change does not call forth countervailing changes but, instead, supporting changes, which move the system in the same direction as the first change but much further. Because of such circular causation a social process tends to become cumulative and often to gather speed at an accelerating rate.

A social process can, of course, be stopped. One possibility is that it so happens that new exogenous changes occur which have the direction and the strength that are necessary to bring the system to rest. The position of balancing forces which thus becomes established is, however, not a natural outcome of the play of the forces within the system. The position is, furthermore, unstable. Any new exogenous change will by the reactions in the system again start a cumulative process away from this position in the direction of the new change.

Alternatively, the position of rest may have been achieved by

policy interferences, planned and applied with the intention of
stopping the movement. This is, of course, the very opposite of a
natural tendency toward equilibrium, endogenous to the system.

This general characterization of a process of social change refers
to the normal case; I shall be discussing at the end of the next
chapter the exceptions where countervailing tendencies are at work.

An Illustration: the Negro Problem in America

I once carried out a comprehensive study of the development
problem of one particular group of people: the Negro population in
the United States.[4] It was during this study that I first came to
realize the inadequacy of the equilibrium approach and to understand that the essence of a social problem is that it concerns a
complex of interlocking, circular and cumulative changes. I was
gradually moved to make this thought the main hypothesis of my
study. My purpose in now referring back briefly to this study is to
give greater concreteness to the circular mechanism in a cumulative
process of social change.

The American Negro people are not confined to one single geographic district where they are alone by themselves. But they are,
nevertheless, cut off from the rest of the American population and
are bound together in a distinctly separate social group, with a
community of worries and a common destiny. This relative social
isolation is effected by the American version of the institution of
color caste.

Behind the color line the Negro people live a life almost as
separate as if they were on an island with restricted communications
with the mainland. They have developed an entire class structure of
their own. The caste disabilities reflect themselves in the fact of a
greater concentration of the Negro population in the lower social
strata and also in lower levels of all economic and social indices for
comparable strata. The unity of interests and aspirations in this
social group is just as great as that existing in any underdeveloped
country or region.

[4] *An American Dilemma. The Negro Problem and Modern Democracy,*
Harper, New York, 1944.

The relative status of the Negro people in America in the late thirties and early forties, when I made my survey, had been rising since the great national compromise in the 1870's, after the Civil War and Reconstruction, but not very rapidly, and there had even been some retreats.

The prevailing views on the Negro problem among social scientists were mostly framed in terms of static equilibrium and *laissez faire* and demonstrated rather faithfully the general tendency toward social fatalism which is inherent in this approach. Mistrust of the efficiency of "interferences" with the social process—such as, for example, efforts toward educating the white people to broader views, campaigns for giving Negroes legal redress through the courts, and legislation, "movements" and "reforms"—characterized the approach and was felt to bear the mark of hard-boiled scientific objectivity in contradistinction to the credulity of the do-gooders.[5] The practical conclusion tended to be that the rise in Negro status would continue to be, as it had been for generations, a very slow and uncertain process, largely outside the grip of intentional policy measures: "state-ways cannot change folk-ways." [6]

[5] Nevertheless, the social scientists of this period—though often asserting in all good faith that their findings and teaching could not have any great practical effects on the development of interracial relations in America—were actually all the time efficiently bringing together and organizing the rational arguments for a fundamental social change. Indeed, they were making it increasingly difficult for educated white people to continue to hold some of the stereotyped opportunistic views which were basic to segregation and discrimination. It is my conviction, for which I have given the evidence in the book referred to above, that the work of American social scientists during the prewar period contributed mightily toward producing the driving forces for the dynamic development of interracial relations which began to gather increased momentum some ten years ago.

[6] This laissez-faire approach in the tradition of William Sumner—with still older moorings in the natural law philosophy which, with all the enthusiasm for fact finding, has a particularly strong hold in America—was often connected with a vague philosophy of economic determinism. In the prewar period, it presented itself in two versions with many intermediary positions: a radical Marxist version, where the expectation was an economic revolution which would change everything and even eradicate race prejudice; and, much more commonly, a conservative liberalistic version, according to which no such revolution was to be expected and, consequently—as the assumption in that version too was that no significant change can be brought

In my study I reached the conclusion that the national compromise which had reigned for such a long time was approaching its end. "Ten years from now this (past) period in the history of interracial relations in America may come to look as a temporary interregnum. The compromise was not a stable power equilibrium." [7] More positively, my conclusion was that "not since Reconstruction has there been more reason to anticipate fundamental changes in American race relations, changes which will involve a development toward the American ideals." [8] This great, dramatic break in the social development of American society has since actually happened. A student who has sometimes been wrong in his forecasts of the future will be excused for pointing to a case when he was right.

Circular Causation

I want now to sketch in its barest outlines the social theory or methodological hypothesis that I used in this particular study.[9]

In its simplest form the explanatory model can be reduced to two factors: "white prejudice," causing discrimination against the Negroes in various respects, and the "low plane of living" of the Negro population. These two factors are mutually interrelated: the Negroes' low plane of living is kept down by discrimination from the whites while, on the other side, the Negroes' poverty, ignorance, superstition, slum dwellings, health deficiencies, dirty appearance, bad odor, disorderly conduct, unstable family relations and criminality stimulate and feed the antipathy of the whites for Negroes.

---

about except by tackling the "basic factor," the economic system—the situation would remain pretty well as it was and that, anyhow, there was not much chance for the reformers to alter much. The one-factor theory thus strengthened the equilibrium approach and its inherent fatalistic tendency and stood in the way of a rational conception of circular interdependence leading to a cumulative dynamic development, implying chances also for magnified effects of purposively induced changes.

[7] *An American Dilemma*, p. 1014.

[8] *Ibid.*, p. XIX.

[9] The rest of this section contains a condensation of the methodological argument in the book cited and particularly Chapter 3, Section 7, "The Theory of the Vicious Circle," pp. 75 ff., and Appendix 3, "A Methodological Note on the Principle of Cumulation," pp. 1065 ff.

White prejudice and low Negro standards thus mutually "cause" each other. If at a point of time things tend to remain about as they are, this means that the two forces balance each other: white prejudice and the consequent discrimination against the Negroes block their efforts to raise their low plane of living; this, on the other hand, forms part of the causation of the prejudice on the side of the whites which leads them to discriminatory behavior.

Such a static "accommodation" is, however, entirely fortuitous and by no means a stable equilibrium position. If either of the two factors should change, this is bound to bring a change in the other factor, too, and start a cumulative process of mutual interaction in which the change in one factor would continuously be supported by the reaction of the other factor and so on in a circular way. The whole system would move in the direction of the primary change, but much further. Even if the original push or pull were to cease after a time, both factors would be permanently changed, or even the process of interacting changes would continue without a neutralization in sight.

Both of the two factors are composite entities. On the one hand, the Negro's plane of living is an amorphous concept definable only in terms of a number of components—employment, wages, housing, nutrition, clothing, health, education, stability in family relations, law observance, cleanliness, orderliness, trustworthiness, loyalty to society at large, etc.—which are all interrelated in circular causation. A rise in any single one of the components would tend to raise all the others and thus, indirectly as well as directly, result in a cumulative decrease in white prejudice, with new effects back on the Negro plane of living itself.

The other factor, white prejudice, is an equally composite entity, as "attitudes" always are: a combination of right and wrong beliefs and heterogeneous valuations. And it is equally unstable. For experience shows that if, by some chance, discrimination in a particular field of social contact is increased or decreased, the psychological force behind it, i.e., prejudice, tends to change so as to support actual behavior. This too fits into the general patterns of circular causation.

The point is not simply that "many forces are working in the same direction." They are, in fact, not doing so. In general there are periods when opposing forces balance one another so that the system remains in rest until a push or a pull is applied at one point or another. When the whole system starts moving after such a shock, the changes in the forces work in the same direction, which is something different. And this is so because the variables are so interlocked in circular causation that a change in any one induces the others to change in such a way that these secondary changes support the first change, with similar tertiary effects upon the variable first affected, and so on.

The Scientific Problem

The circular causal interrelation among all the factors in the development of a population group like the American Negroes gives sense to the general notion of the "status" of the group—in essentially the same way as the interrelation between prices gives sense to the notion of the "price level"—and an index of this status could be constructed and would have meaning as measuring in time or space the general tendency of the system. The main scientific task is, however, to analyze the causal interrelations within the system itself as it moves under the influence of outside pushes and pulls and the momentum of its own internal processes.

In a realistic study the system becomes, of course, very much more complicated than any abstract model. In the case of the Negro problem, for example, each of the elements of the main factors in the situation—the low Negro plane of living and white prejudice—needs to be studied intensively with reference to other variables such as region, social class, age, sex, and so on. The scientific ideal is not only to split the factors into their elements and arrange them in this way but to give for each of the elements quantitative measures of its ability to influence each of the others, and to be influenced itself by changes in other elements within the system or by changes in exogenous forces.

The outside forces in the study in question are essentially the whole surrounding national community. Some of these outside forces, e.g., the business situation and employment opportunities, are subject to violent short-term changes. Others are more constant determinants, for instance, the complex of inherited ideals that I called "the American Creed" in my study and the institutional and political framework as it is influenced and activated by those ideals. The outside forces push and pull the system continuously and at the same time they change the structure of forces within the system itself.

The time element is of paramount importance as the effects of a shock on different variables of the system will be spread very differently along the time axis. A rise in employment, for instance, will almost immediately raise some levels of living; but a change in levels of education or health is achieved more slowly, and its effects on the other factors are delayed, so that there is a lag in the whole process of cumulation.

Ideally the scientific solution of a problem like the Negro problem should thus be postulated in the form of an interconnected set of quantitative equations, describing the movement—and the internal changes—of the system studied under the various influences which are at work. That this complete, quantitative and truly scientific formulation is far beyond the horizon does not need to be pointed out. But in principle it could be made, and I submit that the working out of such a complete and quantitative solution should be the aim of our less perfect research endeavors.

If the realism of the hypothesis of circular causation is accepted, certain general conclusions can be drawn which it is worth while to spell out already at this point. To begin with, it is useless to look for one predominant factor, a "basic factor" such as the "economic factor." [10] When studying the Negro problem or any other social problem under this hypothesis it becomes, indeed, difficult to perceive what precisely should be meant by the "economic factor" as distinct from the others, and still less understandable how it can be

[10] We might in this connection note that there has been much unconscious application of Marxian economic determinism, particularly in the American sociological literature, sometimes of a kind that Marx and Engels would have been tempted to characterize as "vulgar Marxism."

"basic," as everything is cause to everything else in an interlocking circular manner.

For similar reasons, the application of this hypothesis moves any realistic study of underdevelopment and development in a country, or a region of a country, far outside the boundaries of traditional economic theory. This is because of necessity the study becomes concerned also with all the so-called "noneconomic factors" which the classical economists lumped together in such concepts as "the quality of the factors of production" and the "efficiency of production" and usually kept outside their analysis.

That, if the hypothesis of cumulative causation is justified, an upward movement of the entire system can be effected by measures applied to one or the other of several points in the system is a very important thing to keep in mind. But it certainly does not imply that from a practical and political point of view it is a matter of indifference where and how a development problem is tackled. The more we know about the way in which the different factors are interrelated—what effects a primary change of each factor will have on all the other factors, and when—the better we shall be able to establish how to maximize the effects of a given policy effort designed to move and change the social system.

Nevertheless, it is unlikely that a rational policy will work by changing only one factor. Thus, though this theoretical approach is bound to suggest the impracticability, in the political sphere, of all panaceas, it is, on the other hand, equally bound to encourage the reformer. The principle of cumulation—in so far as it holds true—promises final effects of very much greater magnitude than the efforts and costs of the reforms themselves. The low status of the Negro is, for instance, tremendously and self-perpetuatingly wasteful all round—the low educational standard causes low productivity, health deficiencies and low earnings, and these again keep down the educational standards, and so on.

The cumulatively magnified final effects of a push upward when wisely applied to the relevant factors is, in one sense, a demonstration, and also a measure, of the earlier existing "social waste." In the end, the cost of raising the status of the Negro will not involve any "real net cost" at all, but instead result in great "social gains" for society. The definition of these political concepts, based on explicit value premises, must be conceived of in the dynamic terms of circular causation of a cumulative development.

This is, indeed, the principle by which an underdeveloped country can hope to "lift itself by its own bootstraps"—if it can only manage to accomplish what Professor W. W. Rostow calls the "take-off into sustained growth" [11] and afford the sacrifice of waiting for the full returns of its policy efforts.

Argumentum ad Hominem

I started this chapter by referring to the floating, vague notion of the "vicious circle" and by citing folklore and the Bible. I feel, indeed, very much in line with ordinary common sense when I stress that in the normal case circular causation is a more adequate hypothesis than stable equilibrium for the theoretical analysis of a social process.

John Maynard Keynes had some basis for his famous dictum that usually "the practical men" are unknowingly "the slaves of some defunct economist" when they express general opinions. They then often think in the metaphysical terms of the doctrines and predilections of economic theory. But in their own sphere of activity they act on better assumptions.

Every successful businessman has the principle of the cumulative process as a built-in theory in his approach to practical problems; otherwise he would not be successful. A politician would be a failure if he did not bring the cumulative effects into his calculations. The whole philosophy of the professional philanthropists is imbued with this hypothesis.[12]

[11] W. W. Rostow, "The Take-off into Sustained Growth," *Economic Journal,* 1956, pp. 25–48.

[12] In fact, the best formulation I have found of the working of the cumulative process in the field of the Negro problem was given by one of the wisest heads of foundations in America, the late Edwin R. Embree of the Rosenwald Fund: "There is a vicious circle in caste. At the outset, the despised group is usually inferior in certain of the accepted standards of the controlling class. Being inferior, members of the degraded caste are denied the privileges and

I go further and feel inclined to think that Keynes's accusation of traditionalism could be directed with even more justice against the economists themselves, particularly since the duty would clearly have been ours to liberate not only our own thinking but also that of the general public.

The practical men have been ahead of theory in monetary matters, to choose a more specific case. It is a fact that the new and dynamic approach, which was opened up by Knut Wicksell, followed by many others—and among them, of course, most prominently Keynes—and which has reshaped such a large part of short-term economic theory as well as economic policy, was totally original only to the theoreticians, with their usually unquestioning acceptance and belief in J. B. Say's law of the necessary equilibrium between total demand and total supply.

The laymen have, of course, never believed in that law; they have always known that demand could fall short of, or exceed, supply, and that in the former case business was booming, while it was falling off in the latter case. And Wicksell's new approach only spelled out in clearer terms vague ideas held by bankers, businessmen and political leaders upon the basis of which they had always been acting—though on a more general plane, where they were only talking and at most demonstrating their prejudices, they usually felt happy to fall in with the false doctrine and predilections of the theoreticians.

---

opportunities of their fellows and so are pushed still further down and then are regarded with that much less respect, and therefore, are more vigorously denied advantages, and so around and around the vicious circle. Even when the movement starts to reverse itself—as it most certainly has in the case of the Negro—there is a desperately long unwinding, as a slight increase in goodwill gives a little greater chance and this leads to a little higher accomplishment and that to increased respect and so slowly upward toward equality of opportunity, of regard, and of status." (*Brown America: the Story of a New Race,* The Viking Press, New York, 1931, p. 200.) The vaguely implied notion that circular causation retards the speed of progress is, however, wrong.

III.

The Drift toward Regional Economic Inequalities in a Country

A Simple Illustration

I HAVE suggested that the principle of interlocking, circular interdependence within a process of cumulative causation has validity over the entire field of social relations. It should be the main hypothesis when studying economic underdevelopment and development.

Suppose that in a community an accidental change occurs which is not immediately canceled out in the stream of events: for example, that a factory, where a large part of the population gets its livelihood, burns down and that it becomes clear that it would not pay to rebuild it, at least not in that locality. The immediate effect of this primary change is that the firm owning it goes out of business and its workers become unemployed. This will decrease incomes and demand.

In its turn the decreased demand will lower incomes and cause unemployment in all sorts of other businesses in the community which sold to, or served, the firm and its employees. A process of circular causation has so been started with effects which cumulate in the fashion of the "vicious circle."

If there are no other exogenous changes, the community will be less tempting for outside businesses and workers who had contemplated moving in. As the process gathers momentum, businesses established in the community and workers living there will increasingly find reasons for moving out in order to seek better markets somewhere else. If they do, this will again decrease incomes and demand. It will usually also change the age structure of the local population in an unfavorable direction.

To throw light on the mechanism of this cumulative causal sequence, let us watch the behavior of one single factor and let us choose one a little outside: the local tax rate. I will assume that local taxation is either, as in Scandinavia, levied directly on incomes or, as in many other parts of the world, indirectly related to them. As the income basis narrows, the tax rate will have to be raised.

The higher tax rate, in its turn, will itself act as an extra incentive for businesses and workers to leave the community and as a disincentive keeping out those who otherwise might have considered moving in. This then, in a second round, will again decrease incomes and demand and, consequently, cause the tax rate to move still further upward, having much similar effects again. Meanwhile the less favorable age distribution will have not only contributed to lower taxable income per head but also raised the relative need for public welfare services.

If in this situation the local authorities, because of the rising tax rate, are moved to lower their standards in various public services —such as the provision of schooling for children, homes for the aged, roads, and the like—the rise of the tax rate may be retarded but only at the expense of making the community less attractive for businesses and workers in another important respect.

Should the tax rate before the first change have reached a stationary level, it is now not moving toward this level as an equilibrium—or any other stable level—but continuously away from the initial state of balancing forces. And this movement itself is all the time causing new changes which push the tax rate still higher, and so on and so on. This simple model of circular causation with cumulative effects, released by a primary change, is, I believe, more typical of actual social processes than the intersection of the demand and supply curves at an equilibrium price which has become symbolic of much of our reasoning in economy theory.

If, nevertheless, in well-organized welfare states the local tax rate does not continue on that adventurous course but is prevented from rising too much, and if also the community is restrained from lowering the standards of public services too much, this has quite another explanation than the play of market forces: namely, the fact that national legislation has been enacted for the specific purpose of stopping such a cumulative process by subsidizing from the common purse any individual community which for reasons outside its own command has got into financial difficulties, and at the same time prescribing certain minimum standards for public services.

Indeed, the modern highly integrated national states in the one-sixth of the non-Soviet world which is well off and rapidly progressing have furnished themselves with a most complex network of systems of regularized public interferences of all sorts which have the common purpose of counteracting the blind law of cumulative social change and hindering it from causing inequalities between regions, industries and social groups. To this question of the counter-vailing changes induced by organized society I shall come back in the next chapter.

In my example the primary change was an adverse one. The cumulative process, however, also works if the initial change is for the better. The decision to locate an industry in a particular community, for instance, gives a spur to its general development. Opportunities of employment and higher incomes are provided for those unemployed before or employed in a less remunerative way. Local businesses can flourish as the demand for their products and services increases. Labor, capital and enterprise are attracted from outside to exploit the expanding opportunities. The establishment of a new business or the enlargement of an old one widens the market for others, as does generally the increase of incomes and demand. Rising profits increase savings but at the same time cause investments to go up still more, which again pushes up the demand and the level of profits. And the expansion process creates external economies favorable for sustaining its continuation.

The local tax rate—the factor I picked out for a closer view of the causal interrelations in a downward cumulative process—can be lowered and the amount and quality of public services enhanced: both changes will make the community more attractive to businesses and workers for this reason also, with the result that the local finances will again be boosted, with similar results on the tax rate and public finances, and so on.

These fiscal effects of localized expansion may be reduced as a result of interferences by the state in the form of schemes for inter-regional equalization built into the taxation system, but as in the present chapter I am still considering only the free play of the market forces I shall neglect this possibility for the moment.

The Play of the Market Forces Works toward Inequality

A cumulative process of the same general character, going downward or upward as the case may be, will also be generated by a change in the terms of trade of a cummunity or a region, if the change is large and persistent enough, or, indeed, by any other change having as its effect a substantial decrease or increase in the interrelated economic quantities: demand, earning power and incomes, investment and production. The main idea I want to convey is that the play of the forces in the market normally tends to increase, rather than to decrease, the inequalities between regions.

If things were left to market forces unhampered by any policy interferences, industrial production, commerce, banking, insurance, shipping and, indeed, almost all those economic activities which in a developing economy tend to give a bigger than average return— and, in addition, science, art, literature, education and higher culture generally—would cluster in certain localities and regions, leaving the rest of the country more or less in a backwater.

Occasionally these favored localities and regions offer particularly good natural conditions for the economic activities concentrated there; in rather more cases they did so at the time when they started to gain a competitive advantage. For naturally economic geography sets the stage. Commercial centers are, of course, usually located in places where there are reasonably good natural conditions for the construction of a port and centers for heavy industry are most often located not too far away from coal and iron resources.

But within broad limits the power of attraction of a center today has its origin mainly in the historical accident that something was once started there and not in a number of other places where it could equally well or better have been started, and that the start met with success. Thereafter the ever-increasing internal and external economies—interpreted in the widest sense of the word to include, for instance, a working population trained in various crafts, easy communications, the feeling of growth and elbow room, and the spirit of new enterprise—fortified and sustained their continuous growth at the expense of other localities and regions where, instead, relative stagnation or regression became the pattern.

Migration, Capital Movement and Trade: the "Backwash Effects"

It is easy to see how expansion in one locality has "backwash effects" in other localities. More specifically the movements of labor, capital, goods and services do not by themselves counteract the natural tendency to regional inequality. By themselves, migration, capital movements and trade are rather the media through which the cumulative process evolves—upward in the lucky regions and downward in the unlucky ones. In general, if they have positive results for the former, their effects on the latter are negative.[1]

The localities and regions where economic activity is expanding will attract net immigration from other parts of the country. As migration is always selective, at least with respect to the migrant's age, this movement by itself tends to favor the rapidly growing communities and disfavor the others.

In the historical epoch—which is only just now coming to its end in the very richest and most advanced countries—when birth control is still spreading to lower economic and social strata,[2] the poorer regions will also have a relatively higher fertility. This adds its influence to that of the net emigration in making the age distribution in these regions unfavorable; in the longer run it may also cause a

---

[1] This statement will be qualified in the section after the next.

[2] When this process is completed, the average fertility might well be rather high or at times even rising; but it is positively, and not negatively, correlated to economic and social status.

less favorable relation between total working population and re-sources. The poverty in rural regions of Europe during the long period of net emigration to the industrial centers—and to America—has a main explanation in the unfavorable age distribution there, caused by migration and in part also by the higher fertility rates.

Capital movements tend to have a similar effect of increasing inequality. In the centers of expansion increased demand will spur investment, which in its turn will increase incomes and demand and cause a second round of investment, and so on. Saving will increase as a result of the higher incomes but will tend to lag behind invest-ment in the sense that the supply of capital will steadily meet a brisk demand for it. In the other regions the lack of new expansionary momentum has the implication that the demand for capital for in-vestment remains relatively weak, even compared to the supply of savings which will be low as incomes are low and tending to fall. Studies in many countries have shown how the banking system, if not regulated to act differently, tends to become an instrument for siphoning off the savings from the poorer regions to the richer and more progressive ones where returns on capital are high and secure.

Trade operates with the same fundamental bias in favor of the richer and more progressive regions against the other regions. The freeing and widening of the markets will often confer such com-petitive advantages on the industries in the already established cen-ters of expansion, which usually work under conditions of increasing returns, that even the handicrafts and industries existing earlier in the other regions are thwarted. The hampering of industrial growth in the poorer southern provinces of Italy, caused by the pulling down of internal tariff walls after Italy's political unification in the nineteenth century, is a case in point which has been thoroughly studied: industry in the northern provinces had such a lead and was so much stronger that it dominated the new national market, which was the result of political unification, and suppressed industrial efforts in the southern provinces.[3]

[3] The process was conditioned and encouraged by the liquidation of the political and administrative centers in southern Italy, while those in northern Italy, which at that time more than now were tools in the hands of the

As industrialization is the dynamic force in this development, it is almost tautological to state that the poorer regions remain mainly agricultural: the perfection of the national markets will even, as I just mentioned, tend to frustrate earlier beginnings of industrial diversification in agricultural regions. In the backward regions of Southern Europe about three-quarters of the population get their livelihood from agriculture. In these regions, also, not only manufacturing industry and other nonagricultural pursuits but agriculture itself show a much lower level of productivity than in the richer regions.[4]

The "Noneconomic Factors"

The cumulative processes toward regional inequality work through many causal chains usually not accounted for in our theoretical analysis of the play of market forces. I have already referred to the selectivity in migration and the effects of poverty on fertility.

If left to themselves, those regions which had not been touched by the expansionary momentum could not afford to keep up a good road system, and all their other public utilities would be inferior,

---

industrial interests there, gained hegemony over the whole country. The unification of Italy was in reality very much a conquest and an annexation to southern Italy by the stronger North. The role of the state in the cumulative process will be discussed in the next chapter.

Another example on a still larger scale is the long economic stagnation after the Civil War up till the Second World War of the Southern states of the United States. As I shall argue in Chapter V, this systematic bias of trade as between regions forms also part of the mechanism of exploitation in the economic relations between a metropolitan country and its colonies.

[4] Part of the stronger competitive position of industry in Northern Italy at the time of Italy's political unification was based on the fact that it also had a more developed agriculture.

Professor Jacob Viner makes the plausible point that ". . . the real problem in poor countries is not agriculture as such, or the absence of manufactures as such, but poverty and backwardness, poor agriculture and poor manufacture" (*International Trade and Economic Development,* The Clarendon Press, Oxford, 1953, p. 52). This is supposed to be a criticism of Professor Raúl Prebisch and others who have urged industrialization as the necessary mainstay in a program of economic development. As his argument is narrowly static, Viner, however, misses entirely the point that industrialization is intended to rectify an economy in imbalance and to give a dynamic momentum.

thus increasing their competitive disadvantages. Railways would be built so as to meet the effective demand for transport, which would imply: without much consideration of the needs of those regions.

On the same assumption the poorer regions, unaided, could hardly afford much medical care, and their populations would be less healthy and have a lower productive efficiency. They would have fewer schools and their schools would be grossly inferior—in Southern Europe the population of the poorer regions is actually still largely illiterate.

The people living there would on the average be believers in the more primitive variants of religion, sanctioning traditional mores by taboos and functional magic, and they would be more superstitious and less rational generally. Their entire systems of valuations would take on such an imprint of poverty and backwardness that they would become even less susceptible to the experimental and ambitious aspirations of a developing society.

All these frustrating effects of poverty, operating through other media than those analyzed by traditional economic theory, are interlocked in circular causation, the one with the others and all with the biases I referred to in the working of migration, capital movements and trade. The opposite effects of rising economic levels in the centers of expansion are in a similar fashion also interconnected in a circular causation, continuously sustaining further expansion in a cumulative fashion.

Economic theory has disregarded these so-called noneconomic factors and kept them outside the analysis. As they are among the main vehicles for the circular causation in the cumulative processes of economic change, this represents one of the principal shortcomings of economic theory. As I pointed out in Chapter II and shall further pursue in Chapter XI, it explains largely why this theory was unable to state the dynamic problems of economic underdevelopment and development—or, to formulate it differently, how this theory managed to avoid stating those problems.

For easy reference I shall refer to all relevant adverse changes, caused outside that locality, as the "backwash effects" of economic expansion in a locality. I include under this label the effects via migration, capital movements and trade as well as all the effects via the whole gamut of other social relations exemplified above, and the term refers to the total cumulated effects resulting from the process of circular causation between all the factors, "noneconomic" as well as "economic."

It should be pointed out in this connection that all history shows that the cheap and often docile labor of underdeveloped regions does not usually attract industry. The few examples where the labor supply has been effective in bringing industry to backward regions—the movement of textile industry from New England to the Upper South in the United States is one case—are rather in the nature of exceptions to a general rule. There are so many forces working in the opposite direction, among them the external economies in the established centers of economic expansion. Ordinarily it is labor which has to move to the localities of rising demand and there make the difficult effort of adjustment to the different ways and values of an expanding society.

The "Spread Effects"

Against the backwash effects there are, however, also certain centrifugal "spread effects" of expansionary momentum from the centers of economic expansion to other regions. It is natural that the whole region around a nodal center of expansion should gain from the increasing outlets of agricultural products and be stimulated to technical advance all along the line.

There is also another line of centrifugal spread effects to localities farther away, where favorable conditions exist for producing raw materials for the growing industries in the centers; if a sufficient number of workers become employed in these other localities, even consumers' goods industries will be given a spur there. These, and also all other localities where new starts are being made and happen to succeed, become in their turn, if the expansionary momentum is strong enough to overcome the backwash effects from the older centers, new centers of self-sustained economic expansion.

The spread effects of momentum from a center of industrial expansion to other localities and regions, operating through increased demands for their products and in many other ways, weave themselves into the cumulating social process by circular causation in the same fashion as the backwash effects in opposition to which they set up countervailing changes. They represent a complication of the main hypothesis that in the normal case the changes in other factors which are called forth as reactions by a change in one factor always tend to move the system in the same direction as the first change.

In no circumstances, however, do the spread effects establish the assumptions for an equilibrium analysis. In the marginal case the two kinds of effects will balance each other and a region will be "stagnating." But this balance is not a stable equilibrium, for any change in the forces will start a cumulative movement upward or downward.

In reality, the expanding, stagnating and regressing localities are arranged in a fairly continuous series on different levels, with all possible graduations between the extremes. In so far as in the aggregate all the dispersed industrial advances amount to something, considerable economic standards in the whole country are given a lift.

It is quite possible that all the regions in a country may be inside this margin of balancing forces—if the initial starts are many and strong and successful enough and if the centrifugal spread effects work relatively effectively. The problem of inequalities then becomes a problem of the different rates of progress between regions in the country. But ordinarily, even in a rapidly developing country, many regions will be lagging behind, stagnating or even becoming poorer; and there would be more regions in the last two categories if market forces alone were left to decide the outcome.

Even in such countries as the United States and Sweden, where in the past century business enterprise was able to exploit a particularly favorable situation as regards natural resources and where other unusually advantageous conditions for economic growth also were present, not least in the general cultural situation, the development was not such as to draw the whole country into a more or less equal and simultaneous expansion process. A closer view reveals great disparities. In the United States, for example, almost the whole of the region usually referred to as the South was until recently largely a stagnating one. Similarly, the emergence some generations ago of the great new opportunities in agriculture on the western frontier left large rural areas in New England in a decay from which some of them have not yet emerged.

A country where, on the contrary, few starts are being made and/or where the starts do not happen to meet with such success that they result in a substantial and sustained increase in demand, incomes, investment and production becomes an underdeveloped country. Even there, however, as in several Latin-American countries, there are usually localities and regions which are advancing industrially.

Two Broad Correlations

The Secretariat of the United Nations Economic Commission for Europe has for several years devoted increasing attention to the empirical study of the problem of regional underdevelopment and development in various European countries. The results so far reached have been published in the annual *Economic Surveys of Europe*. In 1955 a more comprehensive analysis of these problems was contained in a separate chapter of the Survey.[5] From this study I want only to quote two main conclusions.

The first one is that in Western Europe disparities of income between one region and another are much wider in the poorer countries than in the richer ones. If we use such a simple measure of regional inequality as the proportion of the total population of a country living in regions where the average income is less than two-thirds of the national average, we find that this proportion amounted to only a few per cent in Great Britain and Switzerland, to some 10 per cent in such countries as Norway and France, and to about one-third in Italy, Turkey and Spain.[6]

The second conclusion is that, while the regional inequalities have

[5] " Problems of Regional Development and Industrial Location in Europe," *Economic Survey of Europe in 1954,* Geneva, 1955, pp. 136 ff.

[6] Not only the inequalities within each country but also the differences in relative inequality between countries would have appeared much greater, if the administrative division in regions used for the tabulation had been more adequate to the problem studied.

been diminishing in the richer countries of Western Europe, the tendency has been the opposite in the poorer ones.

A large part of the explanation for these two broad correlations may be found in the important fact that the higher the level of economic development that a country has already attained the stronger the spread effects will usually be. For a high average level of development is accompanied by improved transportation and communications, higher levels of education, and a more dynamic communion of ideas and values—all of which tends to strengthen the forces for the centrifugal spread of economic expansion or remove the obstacles for its operation.

The neutralization of the backwash effects when a country reaches a high level of development, where the spread effects are strong, will itself spur on economic development and so become an important factor in the cumulative process. For with the extinction of abject poverty on a larger scale goes a fuller utilization of the potentialities of the human resources in a nation. This is one of the explanations why rapid and sustained progress becomes an almost automatic process when once a country has reached a high level of development.

In contrast, part of the curse of a low average level of development in an underdeveloped country is the fact that the spread effects there are weak. This means that as a rule the free play of the market forces in a poor country will work more powerfully to create regional inequalities and to widen those which already exist. That a low level of economic development is accompanied as a rule by great economic inequalities represents itself a major impediment to progress. It tends to hold the underdeveloped countries down. This is one of the interlocking relations by which in the cumulative process "poverty becomes its own cause."

I cannot overcome the temptation to repeat my quotation from the Bible: "For unto every one that hath shall be given, and he shall have abundance: but from him that hath not shall be taken away even that which he hath." That there is a tendency inherent in the free play of the market forces to create regional inequalities and that this tendency becomes the more dominant the poorer a country is are two of the most important laws of economic under-development and development under *laissez faire*.

In this chapter I am abstracting from interferences by the state. In the next chapter, where I discuss the role of the state, my general point is that the activity of the state will tend rather to support those forces which result in the two broad correlations which I have been discussing.

Examples of Other Counteracting Changes

There are a great number of complications and qualifications that in a more elaborate analysis would have to be fitted into the model I am outlining of circular causation of a cumulative social process. They are all related to exceptions from the hypothesis that the causation is circular.

If there are counteracting changes, the cumulative effect will be weakened and the process may even be stopped altogether. But even in the accidental event that the forces come to balance each other the assumption for an equilibrium analysis will ordinarily not be established, for the balance will be unstable. On both sides of such a fortuitous balance the system will entail a cumulative process in the causation of which, however, not all changes are unidirectional and connected.

Among counteracting changes there are those which may be recognized as "external dis-economies," if the term be allowed. There may be factors inherent in the situation of a center of economic expansion which tend to retard or, when it has reached a certain level of development, even to reverse the cumulative process by causing an increase in public expenditure and, perhaps, in private costs because industry and population become too concentrated. Once again this can be stated in the more homely terms of folk wisdom: "Trees can never grow as high as heaven."

To the same category would belong the depressing effects of decreasing demand in a "maturing economy," if this pessimistic theory, cultivated during the Great Depression, particularly in America, were correct—which, however, I doubt, except in very special circumstances.

It may also be that in a center of expansion wages and the re-
munerations of other factors of production will be driven up to such
a high level that other regions get a real chance to compete successfully. Or a prolonged period of economic expansion may have
saddled a prosperous region with a very large stock of old capital
equipment which it is tempting not to discard rapidly, as would be
advantageous in a period of swift technological development. Moreover, a country which, thanks to an early start, has for some time
enjoyed a quasi-monopolistic position may find that the spirit of
enterprise and risk-taking has been damaged.[7]

In the opposite case, a downward cumulative process may also
give rise to endogenous countervailing forces and come to a halt.
The cruel Malthusian checks of classical population theory—a rise
in death rates when population increase had pressed down consumption below the subsistence level—were examples of such countervailing changes. These checks set a limit beyond which regression could
not proceed and thus established a lower limit to the process.
Assuming a permanency in the forces operating in the direction of
economic regression, equilibrium at this low level would indeed for
once be a stable one. The recent explosive development of medical
science, making the prevention of death even at exceedingly low
standards of living a rather easy and inexpensive matter, has tended
to weaken the population checks and thus has moved the stagnation
equilibrium to a much more depressed level of human misery.

Naturally, in the short run, in all countries and in all regions at
all times the equilibrating interplay of countervailing changes in
demand, supply and price—to which economic theory has devoted
such a disproportionate amount of attention—will be operating
more or less according to that theory. This interplay, however,
usually represents only the ripples on the surface.

In general, changes of anticipations consequent on more primary

[7] An analysis of these and other factors which may retard expansionary
movements, as they operated in Europe in the period between the two world
wars, is contained in Professor Ingvar Svennilson's *Growth and Stagnation in
the European Economy,* United Nations Economic Commission for Europe,
Geneva, 1954.

changes tend rather to push a cumulative process in the same direction; this agrees with the main hypothesis. Thus, already an expectation on the part of the white population that the Negro plane of living will rise normally tends to decrease white prejudice. In certain regions of the South in America and, in particular, among the poor whites who compete most closely with the Negroes, such an expectation may instead, at least for a time, cause rising resentment and increased prejudice, which then introduces an opposite secondary reaction but, of course, no equilibrium.

When rising prices cause people to expect further price increases, this will normally induce them to buy more and sell less, so that the primary tendency of the prices to rise will be strengthened, and this agrees with our hypothesis of circular causation. Indeed, it was mainly to the part played by anticipations in the cumulative movement of an economy away from price stability that Wicksell attributed the acceleration of the process in its later stages.[8] But, of course, it is possible that people are so conditioned by theory or earlier experience that they will expect that after a rise in prices there will follow a fall; this then, of course, has the contrary effect.

A realistic study of any social process will have to reckon with a great variety of differently interrelated changes in response to a primary change, and I do not deny that sometimes those changes are interlinked in such a way as to counteract each other. Nevertheless, I believe that when main trends over somewhat longer periods are under consideration the changes will in the main support each other, and thus tend to be cumulative in their net effects.

Changes in General Business Conditions

It has to be remembered, however, that long-term changes are nothing more than the cumulative results of a succession of short-run changes, among which are the short-term fluctuations in the general business conditions of a country. A boom implies a generalized spur to expansion over the whole economic field. It will perhaps

[8] Wicksell's policy goal of a constant price level was not to be expected as an outcome of the play of the forces in the market but as a result of intentional monetary policy.

usually have its most powerful effects in the established industrial centers but may induce a number of new starts in other localities or encourage lagging activity—the result of earlier starts which were losing momentum—to continue. A boom will probably always increase the relative strength of the spread effects. A depression will have the opposite result.

Changes in general business conditions are traditionally dealt with as "the business cycle problem," and this tradition has continued long after these changes seem to have lost every appearance of being cyclical. This is, of course, due to our recognition that there are in the system self-generating changes of the countervailing type, though not combined in the same time space, and this is also my reason for referring to the problem in the present section. Business cycle research has been dominated by the time series: interest has been focused on the aggregate changes from one point or period of time to another, while abstracting rather much from the differences in geographic space and even the changes in time of these special differences.

I believe that more intensive research on the changes in general business conditions focused more specifically on their consequences for economic development would be rewarding. This would imply research on the differences between localities and regions, as those differences change under the influence of the play of the forces in the market during changes in the general business conditions.

IV.

The Role of the State

Egalitarian State Policies in the Richer Countries

IN THE preceding chapter I referred to a recent study of regional underdevelopment and development in Western Europe and stressed two main conclusions from the study:

That regional inequalities are much wider in the poorer countries than in the richer ones; and

that while regional inequalities have been diminishing in the richer countries, the tendency has been the opposite in the poorer countries.

I brought forward as an explanation of these two broad correlations the fact that the spread effects, being themselves a function of the level of economic development actually attained, will be stronger in the richer and weaker in the poorer countries. Under *laissez faire* this would tend to make the inequalities in the poorer countries bigger and increasing. It would be possible to conceive a situation where in a very rich country the spread effects would on the average be stronger than the backwash effects, with the result that inequalities would actually be diminishing as an effect of the play of the market forces.

Of equal importance for the explanation of the two broad correlations is another fact, namely, that without exception all the richer countries in Western Europe have in recent generations been approaching the "welfare state." In these countries state policies have been initiated which are directed toward greater regional equality: the market forces which result in backwash effects have been offset, while those resulting in spread effects have been supported.

In the poorer countries, on the other hand, there has been less of such policies and the market forces have been given freer play—and we recall that, as the spread effects are weaker there as a rule, they are more forceful in creating regional inequalities. In many of the poorer countries the natural drift toward inequalities has been supported and magnified by built-in feudal and other inegalitarian institutions and power structures which aid the rich in exploiting the poor.

In explaining why the richer and the poorer countries have this difference in state policies, we have again to point to circular causation. For one thing, the poorer countries have remained poor partly because in recent generations the efforts to institute national integration policies have been weak, while, on the contrary, the richer countries have succeeded in maintaining their economic progress by carrying out such policies more forcefully. Again, as with the spread effects, it is a question of using more or less fully the human resources of a country.

The egalitarian policies of the modern welfare state are not inexpensive. To the benefits received by the poorer regions in a country correspond sacrifices for the richer regions, at least temporarily. Egalitarian policies therefore meet with greater difficulties in a poorer country, although it needs them more because the weakness of the spread effects has created greater inequalities. This is yet another example of circular causation in the cumulative process: again "poverty becomes its own cause."

In the richer countries, on the other hand, economic progress and rising levels of income mean more elbow room for everybody and therefore give more force to the ideals of rational generosity. When people are better off and have greater security they feel freer to give up privileges and to let down barriers which keep others out and are more prepared to carry the costs of common burdens. And this process, in its turn, strengthens the foundation for continuous economic progress.

In the system of causation the two types of influence—market forces and policies—are interlocked in still another way. A more effective counteraction of the backwash effects by stronger spread effects—and, consequently, less of a tendency to regional inequalities—gives a firmer political basis for egalitarian policies. As, in their turn, those policies result in greater equality, democracy becomes more firmly based as it develops. In the opposite case, to the weakness of the spread effects in a poor country correspond greater economic inequalities: this is inimical to the growth of an effective democracy which could form the power basis for the egalitarian policies such as a country particularly needs, precisely because of the relative weakness of the spread effects and the strength of the backwash effects.

Generally speaking, on a low level of economic development with relatively weak spread effects, the competitive forces in the markets will, by circular causation, constantly be tending toward regional inequalities, while the inequalities themselves will be holding back economic development and at the same time weakening the power basis for egalitarian policies. A higher level of development will strengthen the spread effects and tend to hamper the drift toward regional inequalities; this will sustain economic development and at the same time create more favorable conditions for policies directed at still further decreasing regional inequalities. The more effectively a national state becomes a welfare state—motivated in a way which approaches a more perfect democracy and having at its disposal national resources big enough to carry out large-scale egalitarian policies with bearable sacrifices on the part of the regions and groups that are relatively better off—the stronger will be both the urge and the capacity to counteract the blind market forces which tend to result in regional inequalities; and this, again, will spur economic development in the country, and so on and so on, in circular causation.

These statements are broad generalizations, as a "theory" is permitted to be. They grasp the social facts as they organize themselves into a pattern when viewed under a bird's-eye perspective. The special characteristics and circumstances of every country, every region and, indeed, every acting individual—differences in natural resources and their dispersal in a country, international relations, historical traditions in regard to production activity, national and group cohesion, religions and ideologies, and economic, social and political initiative and leadership, etc.—will result in elaborate variations on the theme. They can, however, all be fitted into this general view of circular causation in a cumulative sequence, while they cannot be integrated into our inherited theories dominated by the equilibrium approach and the distinction between "economic" and "noneconomic" factors.

The "Oppressor State"

The term "state" is used here to include all organized interferences with the market forces. The defense for this terminology is the fact that in modern times the state has in fact become the main manifestation of this organized society and has established itself as the controlling framework for practically all the interferences by other institutions and power groupings within a country.

The traditional role of the "state" in this inclusive sense was mainly to serve as a means for supporting the cumulative process tending toward inequality. It was the economically advancing and wealthier regions and social groups which were the more active and effective in organizing their efforts, and they usually had the resources to stop organizational efforts by the others. And so the "state"—which stands here for organized society—usually became their tool in advancing their interests.

Feudalism was a huge collusion between the rich and mighty to lay a hold on the land and seize power to tax the peasants. The cities enforced their "privileges" upon the surrounding rural regions: the merchants and industrialists in the cities protected themselves against competition from outside. In the cities the richer classes protected themselves effectively against the poorer: labor regulations, not only in the mercantilist state but much earlier, were weighted against the workers and their general purpose was to keep down wages and to keep up the supply of labor.

The heavy antistate and antiorganization bias of the classical economists was thus in their time more of a truly "liberal" position. Their whole theory was built up in protest against the preindustrial state which can in general be characterized as an "oppressor state."

The early stages of the industrial revolution saw the breaking down of many of the regulations of the "oppressor state," protecting the rich against the poor. But for a long time the result was not a development toward greater economic equality. Study of the miserable living conditions of the workers in the early stages of industrialization served as a basis of the revolutionary doctrines of Marx and Engels and was also the source of indignation and inspiration for Dickens, Zola, and a host of other social novelists of the nineteenth century.

In the predemocratic, individualistic age of early capitalism, keeping living standards low for the masses of people was the means of creating the large-scale saving and capital formation which was necessary for rapid economic development. With the spur to accelerated population increase, which occurred at that time, and the technical advances in agriculture, which released labor, the supply of labor became so large that the holding down of wages could be accomplished without the mercantilist regulations: simply by releasing the market forces.

The Long History of Policies for Economic Development of Underdeveloped Regions

But it should not be overlooked that even in the poorest and least progressive countries policy actions were all the time taken by the state to counteract the tendencies toward inequality.

The underprivileged groups pressed for greater equality. From time immemorial, history records uprisings of the poor against the rich, the exploited countryside against the city, the peasants against the landlord. When successful, these revolts by the underprivileged received the sanction of the state.

In Sweden centuries ago "land reforms" were pressed through time and time again, often more radical than those at present carried out or planned in underdeveloped countries. The proud words of the Swedish Constitution—which in free translation may be given in the following form: "The right of the Swedish people from the most ancient time to be taxed only with its free consent is exercised by Parliament"—refer to this important and rather singular historical fact that in Sweden the claims of feudal lords were at all times continuously nipped in the bud by the revolts of the farmers, who thus retained through the centuries fairly intact property rights to the land and thereby also their freedom as citizens.

From the earliest times national states, when they came into being, almost always relied partly upon popular appeal and therefore almost always exerted a certain amount of countervailing power against the tendency to regional inequality. Every national state took some responsibility for common services and for building roads and raising the level of technology in the backward regions— though ordinarily in a poor country a disproportionate part of the meager public funds devoted to such purposes served the richer regions.

In the planning of railways, considerations of short-term profitability, as I mentioned, worked to the advantage of the richer regions. But from the beginning in most countries another purpose also was operative, namely, to open up underdeveloped regions, and freight rates took this into account to some extent. The same applies to the building of electrical power stations and distribution networks. As the banking system developed, some precautions were often taken rather early in the laws regulating this activity to preserve a measure of control over capital resources in the interest of the less industrialized regions; later on specialized financial institutions were established and subsidized to serve their particular credit needs.

As the revolution in ocean transport exposed the European farmers to severe competition, with the result that those engaged in agriculture tended to be remunerated much less generously than other workers, protection for the price of agricultural products was built into the system of economic policies of many countries. Measures to aid the starting of new industries in stagnant regions and to protect existing ones were common in almost all countries from a still earlier stage. In some countries the beginnings of legislation to protect tenants against absentee landowners and farmers against the big corporations, formed to exploit the water power and the forests, also were made long ago.

These policies were weak, particularly in the now poorer and relatively stagnating countries, and for a long time usually were much more than outweighed by other policies framed to favor the richer regions. But they were always present in some measure. In fact, policies for the economic development of underdeveloped regions are as old as the national states themselves.

The main vehicles for these strivings toward regional equalization measures were the national parliaments. As they developed and gradually afforded a platform for grievances, this policy trend gathered momentum. The poor are the many and even the relatively poor are the great majority, wherever the voting line is drawn. In order to gain power political parties had to sponsor reforms in the interest of greater regional equality; this became the more necessary as later the electorate was gradually enlarged.

Popular movements and interested organizations played their important role. Individuals from the privileged classes went over to the other side and contributed leadership to the poor. The more advanced states perfected more and more complicated systems of laws and regulations favoring the poorer regions and the poorer classes generally.

A considerable part of the equalizing measures took the form of transferring ever more functions to be provided for out of the public purse and of transferring the financial responsibility, partially or entirely, to ever larger units: from the local community to the province and from both to the state. This happened gradually to road building and road upkeep, to the provision of clinics and hospitals, to the responsibility for sanitation, for health protection, for education. At the same time minimum standards for public services provided by the municipalities were enforced, and schemes designed to mitigate inequalities as between provinces and communities were embodied in the general tax system, usually considerably earlier than progressive taxation. The institutions to provide professional training, better market outlets, credit and the like for the poorer regions proliferated and were made stronger.

Already a little more than half a century ago there began in the advanced countries the development toward social security reforms, and a couple of decades later toward progressive taxation, two mighty policy trends which have forcefully contributed to equalization even as between regions.

I believe it would be a rewarding task to make an intensive comparative historical analysis of this development in the richer countries from the "oppressor state" to the "welfare state" from the main viewpoints of its interrelation with economic progress and its character of being a part of a cumulative social process. There would be many individual differences as between the several countries, particularly in regard to timing, but I believe that the main conclusion would nevertheless be that the broad patterns of historical sequence were fundamentally similar as well as the circular causal mechanism of social, economic and political factors making the process cumulative.

In the main the trend has been in the direction of greater equality of opportunity and this trend has all the time been related to a rising level of economic development. But in the predemocratic stage of early capitalism the rapid increase of labor supply and other circumstances caused wages to remain low while profits were flourishing, providing for the large savings necessary for the rapid development.

It can be argued that at that stage the inequalities were a necessary condition for progress and perhaps also the lack of political democracy which made their continuation possible. In a lecture on Democratic Values, Aneurin Bevan, after having stressed that "democracy as we know it today is a product of the twentieth century," continued: "It is highly doubtful whether the achievements of the Industrial Revolution would have been permitted if the franchise had been universal. It is very doubtful because a great deal of the capital aggregations that we are at present enjoying are the results of the wages that our fathers went without." [1] Even if

[1] *Democratic Values,* Fabian Tract No. 282, London, 1950.

this were true historically, for a transitional period, a parallel course in those underdeveloped countries which are now planning economic development might not be necessary, or desirable, or even possible. To this question I shall return in Chapter VII.

A "Created Harmony"

In a very few countries we have by now reached a situation where no large social groups and, consequently, no regions are permitted to be really poor and, even more important, where the opportunities for the newly born are becoming more and more equal.

As I pointed out, this implies among other things that the productive powers of the entire population are brought nearer to their real potential. The reforms as they have evolved have at every point of time continuously contributed to raising what the classical economists called "the quality of the factors of production." By thus raising the level of national productivity the reforms have themselves provided the additional resources required for making them economically feasible and for securing at the same time further continued social reform policy.

A main explanation of why these few countries can now be characterized as highly integrated is to be found in these complex networks of systems of state interferences, preventing any region, industry or social group from lagging far behind in its development. The interferences get their support from the sentiment of national solidarity in countries where the ideals of liberty and equality have been operative social forces. The gradual realization of these ideals has in its turn strengthened them and thereby the basis of solidarity for national policy.

Economic progress has supported the spread effects of expansionary momentum, hampered the trend toward inequalities, and thus also solidified the basis for democracy. It has at the same time created the easier conditions for mutual generosity which made the enactment of the equalizing state policies gradually more possible. In its turn the greater equality of circumstances in these countries has sustained economic progress.

Thus policies for national integration, including regional equalization, themselves represent only a phase of the cumulative social process of economic development—though this process has to be conceived of as of a higher order since it includes also, in addition to the evolution of the market forces, people's political attitudes, interferences by the state and, in fact, the entire political process. In these countries social and economic reforms now develop further by their own momentum as almost incidental to economic progress—which has been, and continues to be, in part due to their results.

The need for "reformers" has diminished as now the reforms come without the necessity to fight for them. The distributional conflicts become minimized and their continuous gradual solution secured by the expected general rise in production. To preserve full employment and spur on the rise in production becomes in an ever more egalitarian society the main policy goal and is commonly shared by all regions and groups.

In some of these countries agreement in basic policy issues has become so great that their internal political life has lost much of its earlier dramatic interest. In this situation political parties, trade and professional organizations, and other pressure groups are busy whipping up public attention to ever pettier interests. In fact, they almost have to do so in order to defend their *raison d'être*. It may seem paradoxical but is a fact that a national community which has proceeded far toward harmony of interests will often show a particularly large amount of mutual dissatisfaction, intergroup squabbles and bickering.

At least superficially this becomes the mark of an advanced state of national integration, i.e., at least so far as people's attitudes are reflected in public discussion dominated by those organized social forces. Even if people's attitudes are effected, to an extent, by what goes on at this level of public controversy, behind all the lamentation there is usually a common recognition of the lack of serious grievances: a quiet contentedness.

If these few countries demonstrate an approach to harmony of individual interests—as, indeed, they very definitely do—this is not the old harmony of natural law, utilitarianism and the economic equilibrium theory, brought about by natural forces in the market. It is to a large extent a "created harmony," created through policy interferences by organized society with the operation of market forces which, if left to themselves, would have led to disharmony. And the approach to harmony of interests is narrowly restricted to the nation. The welfare state is nationalistic.

The Price System

One closing word on the operation of the price system. In the highly integrated national states the conditions under which the price system operates have, in this cumulative social process, been radically influenced by the legislation and administration of the state, by the organizations of different interests of all sorts which, in those countries, tend to become quasi-public institutions, and by individual private businesses which, contrary to the assumptions of the theory of price formation under free competition, are powerful enough to influence demand or supply and, consequently, prices.

Prices are manipulated. They are not the outcome only of the forces in the market; they are in a sense "political prices," depending also on the regulating activity of the state, of quasi-public and private organizations, and of private businesses. The state interferences in the price system are, in a sense, the ultimate ones as, under the direction of the political process in a democracy, they are framed to regulate, offset or support the nonstate interferences in order to make the total outcome correspond to the valuations and objectives which emerge from the democratic political process.

Within this institutional framework the price system functions, and apparently quite satisfactorily. It can even be stated that it is precisely in these countries that the price system is given a real chance to function, and function well. In the less well-integrated countries, on the other hand—where the spread effects are weaker and where, furthermore, the state allows freer play to the "natural" forces and has, in fact, because of the general poverty so much less scope for policy interferences—even short-term changes are continuously liable to start a development toward some sort of public disaster.

V.

International Inequalities

Assumptions for the Analysis

IN THIS chapter, in which I deal with the problem of international inequalities, I shall, as in the preceding two, be interested only in the broadest structure of essential facts and causal relations, not, at this stage, in particular cases. The general theory of underdevelopment and development for which I am reaching should explain those facts and relations which are common and essential. It should have, at the same time, the capacity to encompass in successive stages of concreteness the special circumstances of individual underdeveloped countries.

My main hypothesis throughout is that normally a social process is cumulative because of circular causation. I begin by assuming a sort of *laissez faire* in the sense, first, that there are no interferences with the play of the market forces from an organized world community and, second, that national policies in the underdeveloped countries are not different from what they traditionally have been in very poor countries. Toward the end of the present chapter I shall discuss the realism of the first assumption, and in the next two chapters deal with the problem of national state policies and economic planning.

The discussion in the preceding two chapters of the problem of regional inequalities within individual countries is relevant to the present analysis of international inequalities for two reasons. First, to a large extent the two problems are similar. Second, the internal

inequalities in the very poor countries are of paramount relevance
for the international inequalities between countries. As we shall see,
the two types of inequalities are a cause of each other in the circular
way of the cumulative process.

We have seen that within the national boundaries of a very few
of the richest countries an integration process has taken place which
is now being carried forward toward a very high level of equality of
opportunity for all in whatever circumstances they happen to be
born. This development is a joint result of the strong spread effects
and the egalitarian policies in the richer countries. Both these main
factors are in circular causation interwoven with each other and
also with economic progress and a high level of development.

All the countries outside this small group of rich and progressive
countries are in varying degrees poorer and usually less progressive
economically as well. They are ridden by internal economic inequalities, which also tend to weaken the effectiveness of their system of democratic government in the cases where they are not
under one form or another of oligarchic or outright dictatorial rule.

The relations between relative lack of national economic integration and relative economic backwardness run both ways. To a low
level of economic development correspond low levels of social mobility, communications and popular education; this implies greater
impediments to the spread effects of expansionary momentum. At
the same time the poorer nations have for much the same reasons
and because of the very fact of existing internal inequalities often
been less democratic and, in any case, have, because they are
poorer, been up against narrower financial and, at bottom, psychological limitations on policies seeking to equalize opportunities. In
addition, inequality of opportunities has contributed to preserving
a low "quality" of their factors of production and a low "effectiveness" of their productive efforts, and this has hampered their
economic development.

The Effects of Trade, Capital Movements and Migration

On the international as on the national level trade does not by itself necessarily work for equality. It may, on the contrary, have strong backwash effects on the underdeveloped countries.

A widening of markets often strengthens in the first instance the rich and progressive countries whose manufacturing industries have the lead and are already fortified by the surrounding external economies, while the underdeveloped countries are in continuous danger of seeing even what they have of industry and, in particular, small-scale industry and handicrafts priced out by cheap imports from the industrial countries, if they do not protect them.

Examples are easy to find of underdeveloped countries whose entire culture has been impoverished as trading contracts with the outside world have developed. In Bagdad, for example, of the old handicrafts for which the city was famous there survive only a few silversmiths who themselves have adopted patterns from abroad requiring less craftsmanship. Similarly, it is only with the greatest difficulties that one can buy a book of Arabic literature, while cheap magazines in English or Arabic abound.

The main positive effect of international trade on the underdeveloped countries was in fact to promote the production of primary products; and such production, employing mostly unskilled labor, has come to constitute the bulk of their exports. In these lines, however, they often meet inelastic demands in the export market, often also a demand trend which is not rising very rapidly, and excessive price fluctuations. When, furthermore, population is rapidly rising while the larger part of it lives at, or near, the subsistence level—which means that there is no scarcity of unskilled labor—any technological improvement in their export production tends to transfer the advantages from the cheapening of production to the importing countries. Since the demand is often inelastic, the market will not be greatly enlarged.

The advice—and assistance—which the poorer countries receive from the richer is, even nowadays, often directed toward increasing their production of primary goods for export. The advice is certainly given in good faith, and it may even be rational from the short-term point of view of one underdeveloped country seen in isolation. In a broader perspective and from a long-term point of view, what would be rational is above all to increase productivity, incomes and living standards in the larger agricultural subsistence sectors, so as to raise the supply price of labor, and in manufacturing industry. This would engender economic development and raise incomes.

But trade by itself does not lead to such a development; it rather tends to have backwash effects and to strengthen the forces maintaining stagnation or regression. Economic development has to be brought about by policy interferences by the world community or by the individual underdeveloped country—two possibilities which are outside our purview at this stage of the argument when we are analyzing only the effects of the play of the market forces.

Nor can capital movements be relied upon to counteract international inequalities. In the circumstances described, capital will, on the whole, shun the underdeveloped countries, particularly as the advanced countries themselves are rapidly developing further and can offer to owners of capital both good profits and security.

The capital which in earlier times found its way to the countries we today call underdeveloped went to the economic enclaves, controlled from abroad and mainly devoted to the production of primary products for export. They were usually so profitable to their owners that they rapidly became self-supporting so far as investment capital was concerned. A somewhat larger capital export went to investments in railways and other public utilities made secure by the political controls of colonial governments. The bulk of European overseas capital exports went, however, to the settlements in the open spaces in the temperate zones which were becoming populated by emigration from Europe.

After the collapse, which has not been remedied, of the international capital market in the early thirties and later the breakdown of the colonial system, which had given security to the foreign investor, it would be almost against nature if capital were to move voluntarily on a big scale to underdeveloped countries. True, capital is scarce in these countries. But the need for it does not represent an effective demand in the capital market.

Rather, if there were no exchange controls and if, at the same time, there were no elements in their national development policies securing high profits for capital—i.e., if the forces in the capital market were given unhampered play—capitalists in underdeveloped countries would be exporting their capital. Even with such controls and policies in existence, there is actually a steady capital flight going on from underdeveloped countries which, in a realistic analysis, should be counted against what there is of capital inflow to them.

Labor migration, finally, can be safely ignored as a factor of importance for international economic adjustment as between underdeveloped and developed countries. The population pressure in most underdeveloped countries implies, of course, that they do not need immigration, and the consequent low wages that immigrants are not tempted to come. Emigration from these countries would instead be the natural thing. But for various reasons emigration could not be much of a real aid to economic development, even if it were possible.

And it is not possible. The whole world has since the First World War gradually settled down to a situation in which immigrants are on the whole not welcome. By and large, tourism apart, people have to stay in the country where they were born. And so far as the larger part of the underdeveloped world is concerned, where people are "colored" according to the definition in the countries which are white or white-dominated and at the same time better off economically, emigration is usually stopped altogether by the color bar set up either by the legislation or in the administration of those countries.

The Weak Spread Effects

Emigration, therefore, offers no serious prospect of relief to the poorer countries. And, if left unregulated, international trade and capital movements would be the media through which economic progress in the advanced countries would have backwash effects in the underdeveloped world. The mode of operation of these effects would be very much the same as it is in the circular cumulation of causes in the development process within a single country as analyzed in Chapter III. Internationally, however, the backwash effects of trade and capital movements would dominate the outcome much more, as the countervailing spread effects of expansionary momentum are so very much weaker.

To begin with, differences in legislation, administration and mores generally, in language, in basic valuations and beliefs, in levels of living, production capacities and facilities, make national boundaries much more effective barriers to the spread of expansionary momentum than any demarcation lines within one country can be.

Even more important as impediments to the spread effects of expansionary momentum from abroad than the boundaries and everything they stand for are the very facts of great poverty and weak spread effects within the underdeveloped countries themselves. When, for instance, international trade and shipping make the immediate surroundings of a port a center of economic expansion, which happens almost everywhere in the world, the expansionary momentum does not usually spread out to other regions of the country. Basically, the weak spread effects as between countries are thus for the larger part only a reflection of the weak spread effects within the underdeveloped countries themselves caused by their low level of development attained.

In these circumstances market forces will tend cumulatively to accentuate international inequalities.

The Economic Impact of Colonialism

Many of the underdeveloped countries were until recently under the political domination of a metropolitan power, and some still are. In addition, almost all those underdeveloped countries which were not colonies were, and many still are, economically dominated from abroad with effects in the economic field which closely resemble those in the colonies themselves.

In judging the economic results of colonialism and foreign economic domination, I think it would contribute to avoiding an irrational heightening of the resentments of these nations if the main thesis of this book were constantly borne in mind; namely, that because of circular causation a tendency toward inequality is inherent in the unhampered play of the market forces, and particularly so when the general level of development is low. Nationally, once a country has reached a higher average level of economic development, this tendency will be offset by the spread effects of expansionary momentum and by national integration policies. Internationally, for reasons just given, the spread effects are much weaker and the cumulative process will more easily go in the direction of inequality if the forces in the market are given their free play.

If the businessmen and governments of colonial powers try to hang on to the commercial advantages of this tendency of the play of the market forces and also of the political and economic power position inherent in colonialism, this is not because of sinister design on their part. It only means that they accept the world as it is, take care of their own interests, and "play the game" as long as it pays, i.e., think and act in the way good and responsible people can be expected to do.

This should not be implied to mean that the behavior of the metropolitan countries and their businessmen was always, and necessarily, to the disadvantage of the dependent countries. In a very real sense the economic activities of the colonizers represented a measure of spread of economic expansion which without the peculiar power relations of colonialism would not have taken place. Thailand, which thanks to jealousies between the colonial powers was left in political independence, did not become more developed than Burma.

The colonial governments built roads, ports, railways, etc.—or provided the conditions of political security and economic profitability without which they would not have been built by private business concerns. Even when, as usually was the case, these enterprises were motivated primarily by the colonial governments' own interests and those of their settlers and business groups, they represented important advances toward creating the conditions for general economic development.

The colonial governments established law and order, a regular civil service, took measures for elementary sanitation and, in some cases, for popular and higher education on a limited scale. These generally beneficial activities of colonial governments and their business people took on a larger scope in the cases where the political domination was a more complete institutional arrangement and endured for a considerable time, as in India or even Indonesia, while they were of smaller consequence in the cases where the domination was less complete and durable, as in the Middle East.

More generally, colonialism implied contacts with the ideas and ideals of the world of the advanced countries. It conferred also higher education and training for administrative and professional responsibility on some, though to an extent differing greatly as between the several colonial empires.

Those former colonies that are now branching out on their own course as independent states have this heritage as a basis for their policies, including their economic development policies. But during the time of dependence these positive accomplishments showed a persistent tendency not to result in much economic development even if, in most cases, the colonies probably had more development than if they had been left to themselves. To explain this we have to reach down to the mechanism of circular causation in the play of the various forces.

The Play of the Forces

A metropolitan country had, of course, an interest in using the dependent country as a market for the products of its own manufacturing industry. If it took special measures to hamper the growth of indigenous industry—which often happened—this was a natural commercial policy of a country which had political domination over another country. Usually such measures, however, were not necessary, as in the absence of protective duties—which the colony was not permitted to impose—the home industry could easily undersell any colonial competitors.

Likewise, the metropolitan country had a clear and obvious interest in procuring primary goods from its dependent territory and even in investing so as to produce them in plenty and at low

cost, thereby exploiting in its own interest the local natural resources and the indigenous cheap labor.

A metropolitan country had also a self-evident interest in monop-
olizing so far as possible the dependent country for its own business interests, both as an export and as an import market. Its control
of trade and payments policy provided a ready means of securing
preferential treatment for them. But in a natural and normal way
it got the protection of its monopolistic interests fortified even more
by the whole structure of legislation and administration and the
entrenched institutional system of business connections which was
gradually built up.

"Enforced bilateralism," as I have called this phenomenon in
another connection, characterized all colonial empires, though in
different degrees. It was a natural result of political and economic
dependency, and it now tends to retain its hold even after political
liberation.

In the metropolitan countries this bilateral tendency was often
idealized as "close cultural and economic ties" to a mother country.
And, as I said, there were very substantial advantages to the dependent country connected with it. But at the end of the process
it must normally mean a considerable economic disadvantage to the
dependent country, as it tends to worsen its terms of trade by re-
stricting artificially the scope of the markets where it buys and sells.

It gives an interesting sidelight on the power situation in the
world up till recently to note, in passing, that when occasionally
this enforced bilateralism was challenged, it was not usually by the
dependent countries themselves but by other industrially developed
countries which demanded open access to their markets as sources
of raw materials and as outlets for their exports of manufactured
goods.

The capital, enterprise and skilled labor a metropolitan country
sent to a dependent country tended for natural reasons to form
enclaves, cut out and isolated from the surrounding economy but
tied to the economy of the home country. Their economic relations
with the indigenous populations were restricted to their employment as unskilled labor. Racial and cultural differences and the

very much lower level of wages and modes of living made strict segregation a natural consequence even within the enclaves themselves.

Segregation hampered the transfer of culture, including technical skills and the spirit of enterprise, to the indigenous population. It is one of the main reasons why these economic starts of colonialism remained enclaves and why the spread of expansionary momentum was extremely weak or altogether absent.

When employment opportunities were expanded in the mines and on the plantations, the new demand for labor was rapidly filled by population increase, which was also spurred on by the unquestionably beneficial policies, referred to above, of preserving internal order and peace and improving sanitation. As the colonizers had an interest in a plentiful labor supply and low wages for their enclaves, they were not prompted to be disturbed by the rapid population increase and lack of real development in the much larger agricultural subsistence economy outside.

A main interest of a metropolitan country was order and social stability. By an almost automatic logic it therefore regularly came to ally itself with the privileged classes in the dependent country; sometimes such classes were created for this purpose. These favored groups were, by and large, primarily interested in preserving the social and economic *status quo* under which they were privileged, and they would normally not press either for a national integration policy, aimed at greater equality within the country, or for progressive economic development in the main subsistence sector of the economy.

From one point of view, the most important effect of colonialism was related to the negative fact that the colony was deprived of effective nationhood and had no government of its own which could feel an urge to take constructive measures to promote the balanced growth of a national economy. True, in most cases it was only the fermenting influences of the changes brought into the colony by the activity of the colonizers which had gradually brought into existence a situation where such aspirations could be in any degree realistic

and reasonable. At that stage, however, lack of political independence meant the absence of a unifying and integrating purpose for
the community—except, at a still later stage, the negative aim of
expelling the foreign rulers.

The country and the people were laid bare and defenseless to the
play of the market forces as redirected only by the interests of the
foreign metropolitan power. This by itself thwarted individual
initiatives, at the same time as it prevented the formation of a
public policy motivated by the common interests of the people.

For all these reasons, colonialism meant primarily only a strengthening of all the forces in the markets which anyhow were working
toward internal and international inequalities. It built itself into,
and gave an extra impetus and a peculiar character to, the circular
causation of the cumulative process.

It had, and in some countries still has, not least in the dependent
countries themselves, its close parallels in certain institutional power
structures within individual countries: the caste system, the racial
and religious chasms, the dependence of the rural regions upon the
richer city and, in the feudal or semifeudal order, the dependence
of the peasants upon the landlord, the merchant, the moneylender
or the tax collector.

Such hardened institutions of inequality are inimical to economic
progress in the individual underdeveloped countries. If they hamper
the spread effects within those countries they inhibit, at the same
time, the spread of expansionary momentum from the advanced
countries abroad. As I have also mentioned, they have offered to
the metropolitan governments a power basis for maintaining
colonialism and, in fact, have been promoted by those governments.
In these intimate ways internal and international inequalities are
inextricably woven together by mutual causation in a circular
fashion.

The Colonial System under Liquidation

In the era of awakened nationalism in the underdeveloped world
the colonial system is now doomed and its liquidation is one of the

most important political avalanches taking place before our eyes. The remnants of the system are bound to disintegrate within a period of time which is very short in the annals of history.

The new nationalism is always, in a sense and to a degree, "democratic" and, in any case, the old alliances with privileged groups interested in the *status quo* do not any longer assure social peace. In the dependencies which still linger the military and other expenses needed to maintain the regime, the costs and losses caused by the popular revolts, and the financial burden of necessary social reforms and investments in economic development take the profitability out of the colonial system and make it instead increasingly a liability to the metropolitan countries.

Even when in a particular case the development has reached a stage where the clear national interest is to get out as smoothly and rapidly as possible there are, of course, special vested interests in the metropolitan countries, sometimes able to infect whole political factions in their parliaments. The settlers and business corporations, who have profits, investments and a whole way of life to lose, will also resist giving up their privileges.

The ideas about this system as a vehicle for a national "civilizing mission" in history, which under the epoch of colonialism had emerged and become a part of the ideological structures and phraseologies of the different metropolitan countries, will for a considerable time be earnestly upheld by writers, statesmen and the common citizens. Fundamentally, these ideas are, however, largely rationalizations of economic interests.

When the profitability of the system is gradually lost and it stands out as an increasingly expensive political luxury, the colonial system is doomed and the national ideologies will be readjusted accordingly. The intellectual leaders in the great humanistic tradition in these countries will instead increasingly be concerned with the eminently practical problem of how the liquidation of the colonial system can be so handled with wisdom and foresight as to cause a minimum of incidental human suffering and in any case to avoid tragedies on a large scale.

The Heritage from Colonialism

When a poor and backward nation becomes politically independent it will find out, even if it did not know before, that political independence most certainly does not mean that it is automatically on the road to economic development. It will still be up against cumulative social processes holding it down in stagnation or regression: the "natural" play of the forces in the markets will be working all the time to increase internal and international inequalities as long as its general level of development is low.

It inherits a large subsistence economy and, in addition, enclaves producing primary goods for exports. To be able to import the capital goods it urgently needs for economic development it will have to press on with this production for export along the established lines. The "enforced bilateralism" is firmly entrenched in the whole business setup. It can only gradually be transferred into a more profitable system of many-sided business relations with the markets of the whole world. As the new government cannot offer the security of political colonialism it will initially have greater difficulties in attracting foreign entrepreneurs and funds from the international capital market.

The one great asset its liberation from colonial domination will have bestowed on it is its liberty to regulate its life according to the interest of its own people. And this new asset, its freedom to interfere with the play of the forces in the markets, will not be remunerative unless put to use in an intelligent and firm manner. This problem I shall touch on in the next two chapters.

Meanwhile, the very struggle for independence has in many cases released spiritual forces for national identification—this necessary first condition for a nation's ability to conceive a national development plan. India is, of course, an outstanding example of this birth of a nation through the fight for independence.

Libya, on the other hand—which obtained its freedom by a decision of the United Nations as an incidental result of the defeat of Fascist Italy in the Second World War—and several countries in the Middle East—which owe their existence as separate states mainly to the balancing jealousies of the West European colonial powers when carving up the Ottoman Empire after the First World War, and whose boundaries are artificial for the same reason—demonstrate the weaknesses consequent on having won nationhood too haphazardly.

It is in this connection that the broadly educational influences from the countries which have successfully established their new nationhood, and begun to form national policies, become so important for the less fortunate ones. It can be observed how during the past ten years the liberation of so many colonial countries and their vehement cravings, and sometimes active planning, for national economic development has, so to speak as by contagion, inspired to new national policy exertions also those underdeveloped countries, notably in Latin America, which had been politically independent, though often in the bonds of economic domination from abroad.

The Absence of a World State

It is here appropriate to recall that in the developed countries regional inequalities have been mitigated and in a few of the richest and most advanced ones almost wiped out of existence by the spread of expansionary momentum and by policy interferences on the part of the national state. The world as a whole shows, however, an appearance which is more similar to the internal situation in one of the least developed countries, where the spread effects are weak and where the state has been less able to counteract by its intentional policy interferences the backwash effects of the play of the market forces directed toward inequality.

The international situation is only much worse and even more hopeless, because we have hardly more than the faintest beginnings of something like an international authority which could perform for the world as a whole the task of the national state in an individual country. If from one point of view the explanation of the existing and ever-increasing international inequalities is the cumulative tendency inherent in the unhampered play of the market forces in a situation where the effectiveness of the spread effects is weak, from another point of view the explanation is the absence of a world state which could interfere in the interest of equality of opportunity.

On a deeper level the explanation is that there does not exist for mankind as a whole that psychological basis upon which such a policy could be founded: the basis of mutual human solidarity. There is nothing on a world scale corresponding to the state of mind within a nation, built upon a certain homogeneity of culture in all regions and social classes and usually, though not always, strengthened by a common language and religion and the concept of racial oneness, which has evolved from a long history of common destiny and has developed continuously in the advanced countries to ever higher levels by the very experience of sharing the responsibility for the national integration policy itself.

During and immediately after the Second World War courageous attempts were made to build up intergovernmental organizations in many fields for the explicit purpose of initiating policies of international economic integration. This activity was born out of the sufferings and anxieties during the war. All felt that the world had to be remade.

The results of these strivings are small, indeed, measured in terms of the hopes once held out to the peoples. But the efforts still continue. And they will continue, because international integration and equality are ideals which no country and, indeed, no responsible human being can ever afford to give up. Intergovernmental organizations, therefore, when once they have come into existence, and however ineffective they become, will never be liquidated in peace time. They are in that sense among the most stable of human institutions. If for no other reason, we need them to console our international conscience.

Many of these organizations are as yet in the main only propaganda forums and, in addition, media for consultations and for diplomatic contacts between governments. Some produce studies of importance to the learned professions and to individual governments. Some also succeed in arranging co-operation between governments in minor technical matters.

The International Bank for Reconstruction and Development

lends some money, and some of this capital stream is directed toward the underdeveloped countries—very small sums, to be sure, at times probably less than the capital some of these countries lose through capital flights or by the gradual repatriation of investments after their political liberation. Most of the international organizations are active in technical assistance, again on a very small scale. There are possibilities that an international institution will be founded for distributing capital aid, though in very small, almost only symbolic, portions. SUNFED—the Special United Nations Fund for Economic Development—is important as an ideal, long before it has been agreed upon between the powers.

Meanwhile the underdeveloped countries are utilizing the international organizations as places where demands can be raised for international action to improve their terms of trade and counteract the disastrous fluctuations in their export returns. But it is improbable that practical agreements on an important scale will soon be reached in this field. The idea of an international control of industrial cartels is also being quietly buried.

If the practical results are thus as yet meager or altogether absent, nevertheless it is of the greatest importance that there now exist international forums where the underprivileged countries can raise their demands for equality of opportunity and express their dissatisfaction with the operation of market forces. Even if present signs are discouraging, the time may come when these beginnings of a world government which are present in our existing international organizations can be gradually strengthened so that they can come to function in ways which are more and more similar to those of the individual national states within their own boundaries.

We should not forget that as late as in the years just before the Second World War hardly any responsible scholar or statesman would have dreamed of the feasibility of that approach to international taxation on a small scale which the United Nations' technical assistance program actually represents.

The judgment holds, however, that in the foreseeable future the corrective policies initiated by intergovernmental organizations will amount to very little: to very much less than the effects of the changes, upward and downward, in the underdeveloped countries' terms of trade which can be expected to occur from year to year.

In this situation the underdeveloped countries are mainly thrown back on their own resources. Their situation is not entirely hopeless. Even in the absence of a world state which could interfere with the play of the market forces in the interest of greater equality, they are now becoming masters over their own economy and can even regulate international trade in so far as their own exports and imports are concerned.

VI.

National State Policies in Underdeveloped Countries[1]

Rising Nationalism

UNDERDEVELOPED countries, utilizing their newly won independent status, can by purposive policy interferences manage to alter considerably the direction of the market processes under the impact of which they have hitherto remained backward. The cumulative nature of these processes, which has pressed them down, holds out, on the other hand, the promise of high returns from their policy efforts, if they manage to plan them intelligently and carry them out effectively. This, however, is a very big "if."

From that point of view, the political independence they have won for themselves, or are now winning, is their most precious asset. It gives them freedom to organize their own lives according to their own interests. In the absence of a world state, their policies have to be nationalistic in the sense that they must be directed with a single-minded intensity to raising their own economic standards and reaching greater equality of opportunity with the rest of the world. It is not up to them, who are the poor, to take into account internationalist considerations, except those that are also in their own interest. The richer countries are not making many real sacri-

[1] This chapter, as the rest of the book, was completed before Egypt's nationalization of the Suez Canal and the sequence of international crises that were released by that event. I have not found reason to make any material changes in the text.

fices either, though in their case it would be in line with the ideals of liberty and equality.

Economic nationalism does not need to be preached to the newly liberated underdeveloped countries. Nationalism, as I have suggested, has an important function to fulfill in welding together the masses and inspiring them to a common purpose and a unified policy, and this becomes even more important in the virtual absence of a functioning world community. But I feel a special responsibility to add the reminder that an economic policy does not become rational simply because it appeals to national feelings, still less because it might be damaging to other nations. It is the more important to stress this as for natural reasons nationalism in the underprivileged countries contains not only positive urges toward growth and welfare at home but also much resentment against those richer countries which have until so recently been using power to hold in check their national aspirations.

There is a simple rule to apply in drawing the line for sane and sound nationalism: an underdeveloped country is well advised to take any and all measures which, on the ground of good reasoning, can be proved to enhance its own economic welfare, but it should carefully avoid policy measures which are not nationally beneficial in their total and ultimate effects. And culturally it has reasons for learning from all the world. It is a policy of self-defeatism, which a poor country least of all can afford, to build up barriers against the richer world's civilization and values.

I give this advice to rational nationalism with a clear conscience, as it is my firm conviction that real success in the underdeveloped countries' nationalist economic policies would bring us nearer, and not further away from, the stage when an integrated world policy, based on international solidarity, could be more effectively attempted. It is poverty itself which keeps levels of culture in the underdeveloped countries low. And, whether we like it or not, solidarity is a state of mind which is not nurtured by condescending compassion for those who are very different from oneself, but develops naturally between equals and near-equals.

It is not the downtrodden Negro in America who overcomes white prejudices and inspires a natural acceptance of his equal human rights but the educated, prosperous and secure Negro—he is more effectively the fighting Negro. It is when the workers in our advanced countries have won and fortified their right to strike that they can enter into collective bargaining on equal terms—and strikes can then become very rare occurrences.

Land reforms were seldom handed down by public-spirited land-lords on their own benevolent initiative but were pressed upon them by the dissatisfaction of land-hungry peasants. And today in our advanced countries the present agricultural price policies have been won as the result of the political power the farmers exert. In the absence of this power the countryside in most of these countries would for long periods have been more poverty-stricken and backward.[2]

Similarly, among nations it is fundamentally a question of achieving a more equal balance of power. All my observations of the functioning of our weak international organizations have brought me to the conclusion that the main cause of their weakness in the present historical stage is international inequality and, more specifically, the exceedingly weak bargaining power of the under-developed countries which formally constitute their majorities though in reality they are dominated by the tiny minority of rich and powerful countries.

[2] Some of these political advantages won by the underprivileged groups in the advanced countries are at the expense of still more underprivileged peoples in underdeveloped countries. This is an example of the fact that, in the absence of a world state, the nations as integrated entities, including their less privileged groups, become interested participants in joint policies which from a broader point of view work toward international inequality and exploitation.

The peoples in Cuba and Java could be a little better off if we in Europe were to waste less labor in growing sugar beet. By protecting our farmers' butter we are giving less of a chance to the producers of the raw materials for manufacturing margarine. The Egyptians cannot be very happy about the United States' way of supporting its cotton growers.

But this does not contradict the point made in the text, where I am simply illustrating how on the national scene solidarity must be based on some equality of political power.

Growth of Solidarity among the Underprivileged Nations

From this point of view—of attaining a world situation in which there would be more of a democratic power balance and thus a stronger basis of solidarity for concerted international action—every development toward solidarity among the underprivileged countries is also a step forward, in so far as this means that they become stronger.

Underdeveloped countries tend to have their main cultural and economic relations and, in fact, most of their communications with one or several industrial countries, while their mutual ties are weak. This is, indeed, a natural outcome of prolonged economic and cultural backwardness, foreign economic domination and, in particular, political colonialism.

It has its approximate parallel in the paucity of close inter-relations within a subjugated class of families and individuals of many static societies, concomitant with the development of fixed client-patron relations to individual members or families of the dominating class. In such a society, as in the world at large, the underprivileged group has to seek its liberation partly by cultivating its own interrelations. By joining hands and pooling what they have of bargaining power, the underdeveloped countries can together gain for themselves consideration which they could not have got individually.

As yet there is almost no practical economic co-operation among the underdeveloped countries and the basis for fostering it is weak, as the initial situation is almost complete absence of economic relations and often of effective transport facilities. But on the more general political plane there is under way a developing solidarity among the underdeveloped countries which is bound to become in time one of the great vehicles of history. These countries have in common the memory of foreign domination and exploitation, the intense realization of poverty and international inequality, and the ambition of rising to fuller participation in the enjoyment of the world's opportunities.

Their collective support of all liberation movements in the

still-dependent countries is already a political reality of considerable significance. In their internal policies they are beginning to learn from each other's experiences and are not taking all their patterns from the developed countries. In time practical economic co-operation within this group also will develop.

As international solidarity grows among the great majority of mankind which is struggling along in the underdeveloped countries, the minority in the developed countries will feel compelled to join by careful steps the majority, which is becoming powerful, in arriving at common policies for common goals.

This is how, under favorable circumstances, I could see world solidarity coming to us and the gradual emergence of a likeness of, or an approach to, the world state. The benevolence on the side of the richer countries will in this respect be a secondary factor—for the simple reason that, except under the urge of some compulsion, our advanced nations are not prepared to give up privileges and make sacrifices for the poorer countries.

No society has ever substantially reformed itself by a movement from above: by a simple voluntary decision of an upper class, springing from its social conscience, to become equal with the lower classes and to give them free entrance to the class monopolies. Ideals and social conscience do play their very considerable role, which should not be forgotten. But they are weak as self-propelled forces, originating reforms on a large scale—they need the pull of demands being raised and pressed for.

When power has been assembled by those who have grievances, then is the time when ideals and the social conscience can become effective.

The Rich and the Poor Countries Moving Apart

To speak in Hegelian terms: the road to international integration must be sought through national integration. The adoption of nationalist policies by the poor countries and an increase of their bargaining power, as a result of these policies and of increased co-operation between them as a group, are a necessary stage in the development of more effective world-wide international co-operation.

The English have, as very often, a simple and colloquial expression for this learned thought: things must get worse before they can get better. As a matter of fact, the national integration which has already taken place in the rich and highly developed countries has itself caused much international disintegration. The approach to national integration in the underdeveloped countries will likewise, in the first instance, increase international disintegration. Only as a perspective into the future can we discern the possibility that the then internally better organized countries may also find the way to closer international co-operation.

This, however, represents only a possibility and a desirable goal to strive for. Another and less fortunate possibility, which cannot be ruled out, would be that the political tension will indefinitely continue to grow between the two classes of nations, as the lower-class nations become more consolidated and at the same time more conscious of their grievances, while this very development might swell the defensive attitudes on the part of the nations in the upper class.

Indeed, as the rich and economically progressive nations are now facing the strivings of the poor and underdeveloped ones for economic development, the easiest manner of using their powers can be specified in a number of negatives. They can decline, and they do decline, capital aid in any considerable quantity. They can refuse, and they do refuse, to participate in intergovernmental actions for stabilization of the underdeveloped countries' export prices, for control over international cartels in the industrial field and in shipping, and for all the other good causes to which their economists and statesmen committed their nations during the Second World War and immediately afterward.

As the major contributors to the budgets of the international organizations the richer countries can keep down, and they do keep down, these budgets and thereby prevent these organizations from being very effective in promoting the concerted actions for which they were created. By their budget controls, by their relative monopoly of *expertise* in most fields and by their greater power to exert influence with the directing officials of the international organizations and, indeed, upon their selection and appointment, they can prevent dangerous initiatives from being taken and studies from being carried out which would challenge the *status quo*. As an analysis of the output of international organizations, particularly in the economic field, would show, the efforts to make them more and more innocuous have usually been successful.

These negative policies correspond to natural tendencies in those nations which are better off and which therefore have vested interests in preserving the *status quo*. Why should they undertake great sacrifices? True, sacrifices can be motivated in the interest of the welfare of the poor people living in the underdeveloped countries. And it can also be argued that they would be conducive to international integration and in line with ideals and even with the long-range national interests of the richer countries as well. But for that type of policy both the psychological solidarity basis among the peoples and the imagination and daring among their political leaders are largely lacking.

At the same time, in their strivings for national integration the underdeveloped countries are bound to take a number of steps which are discouraging the richer countries from any other policies than the negative ones referred to above. In their turn the negative policies of the richer countries compel the underdevelopd countries to take more such steps and also encourage them to be less considerate toward the richer countries in their national integration policies. Again we are facing a situation of circular causation having cumulative effects.

In fact, the national economic policies of the underdeveloped countries must, to a large extent, particularly in the early stages, be directed against those of the richer countries with whom they have traditionally enjoyed the closest economic relations. For these relations represented colonial or quasi-colonial dependence which must be ended. And this, of course, goes against the interests of the countries which had privileges that must now be taken away from them.

A great number of long-established international economic relations have to be broken in this process. In many cases an underdeveloped country will want to nationalize the foreign-owned installations for exploitation of its natural resources. The reasons for a particular policy step in this process of national economic liberation may be strong or weak, sound or unsound. In any case, one effect will almost of necessity be a lessening of international confidence in capital investments in underdeveloped countries and, indeed, confidence in business relations generally with such countries.

I have already noted that to some extent growing nationalism is both desirable and necessary in underdeveloped countries. In their efforts to lift the peoples living there out of apathy and frustration, caused by centuries of economic and cultural stagnation, and to mold them into national social entities, without which no development is possible, the political leaders simply have to use appeals to nationalistic feelings.

And such appeals are usually also very effective. Most underdeveloped countries lack political traditions, stable administration, and an educated citizenry. In many of these countries the peoples are steeped in racial and religious emotionalism. As their inhabitants become conscious of grievances, the nationalistic feelings can easily develop to an intensity which is beyond any rational justification. And to foment these feelings is often the most effective means, and sometimes the only means, of acquiring and keeping political power, which is the first obligation of every politician.

The effect may easily be that the political leaders are virtually compelled to take policy steps against foreign interests which are not motivated by their country's true development interests but only by the intense nationalistic feelings of the people which the leaders have to cater to. And in this very process these feelings are usually prodded toward new heights of intensity. The policy steps and their emotional causation must, in their turn, tend to move the developed countries into still more negative positions. And so, by circular causation, the political gap between the rich and the poor nations may cumulatively widen.

The Powers of the Poor

The richer countries can use, and are using, their powers to be negative: not to aid, not to get capital to move, not to permit the international organizations to become effective in preparing for concerted actions of various sorts in the interests of the underdeveloped countries.

And, of course, they also have recourse to bribes. If the term "bribe" is taken in a wider and not juridical meaning, many essential elements in the old colonial system were in the nature of bribes to individuals and social groups. Attempts in the postwar world to give economic aid with attached political conditions belong to the same category. On the whole, and judging them by their probable more permanent effects, those attempts have not been very successful. The end result seems most often to be feeding popular resentment.

The underdeveloped countries are weak militarily, financially and commercially. Indeed, I have repeatedly referred to their weak bargaining power as one of the fundamental elements of imbalance in the world. In this situation it should not cause surprise when we find poor countries occasionally using that element of real political power which consists in their being capable of making themselves a nuisance of some sort or another, or threatening to do so.

In the "oppressor state," before there was any effectively functioning political democracy, to make a nuisance of himself was always the ultimate defense of the poor man. Thomas Hobbes pointed out that, while any person's actual possibilities to do good were always severely limited, everyone's opportunity to do damage was always immense. On this principle the dissatisfied members of the world community have available blackmailing powers which they will increasingly learn to use to their own advantage, as they rise to national unity out of the long ages of apathy, social chasms and local isolation.

In many cases the people in an underdeveloped country feel that they have been so maltreated by the world as a whole or by a particular country among the richer ones that they will consider themselves right and just in using all political means at their disposal. Emotional nationalism will usually provide what would lack in rational motivation for feeling self-righteous. And the old cynical idea, that any policy which pays is thereby justified, has, of course, been spread effectively to the underdeveloped countries through centuries of Western colonialism, which in regard to the means employed was never very restrained by moral considerations.

The danger that the underdeveloped countries will increasingly resort to blackmailing will naturally be greater the more the richer countries' approach to their development problems remains negative. Only in so far as we could make real advances toward world democracy—implying a growth of international solidarity on the part of the richer nations and a rising trend of international cooperation to equalize opportunities—can we hope that in the longer range the politicians of underdeveloped countries will feel that they can abstain from using their powers of blackmailing the world community. On the other hand, it is equally apparent that nothing can more effectively consolidate the richer countries in their negative attitudes than a few flagrant cases of such blackmailing. Again, we are up against the principle of circular causation having cumulative effects.

Meanwhile, we are rapidly approaching an era in which the richer countries are no longer in a position to use their superior military strength for controlling the countries with relatively less military power, which, on the whole, are also the underprivileged and dissatisfied ones. This big change works undoubtedly toward a more even balance of power in the world. It has not been brought about through the international organizations: it is, indeed, not at all the result of purposive policy but of the blind forces of the technical development. In the atomic age the use of force in international relations is becoming increasingly unpopular among common people in all countries and particularly in the richer countries where the inhabitants have most to lose by conflicts. People there are wary of any action which might bring the danger of a world conflagration.

If one of the richer and militarily more powerful countries in a critical situation tries to back up its pressure upon an underdeveloped country to act in a certain way by flagging a threat to use force, this will nowadays usually prove to be an ineffective gesture, a bluff which will be called. It may then backfire. It can easily break up whatever solidarity among the richer countries there might have existed in the issue at stake. At the same time nothing can be a more powerful urge for the underprivileged nations to close their ranks than such a threat.

And every time a threat is made and not followed up in action something of the magic of power is permanently lost. The use of threats will then be still less effective in the future. But without the threat of force the ultimatums of even big powers lack substance. This development awards tactical advantages to the poorer countries with relatively less military power, particularly if they are a little more reckless than is the average standard in the world.

The dilemma facing the richer countries becomes evident in the case that the government of one of them decides really to use its military superiority. It will then most likely find world opinion mobilized against it and will usually also cause a dangerous split within its own nation. Apart from whatever short-term arrangements in its favor a government might be able to press through by use of force, a certain and permanent result will be the negative one of having consolidated against itself the resistance and hatred of the poorer nations.

The time has long passed when underdeveloped nations could be policed by demonstrations of military power into conforming to the wishes of the richer ones—and this is so independently of what would be rational from a world point of view or corresponding to the legal *status quo*.

A Moral Element

In the rich and highly developed countries there is also always present, as one strand of opinion among others, anticolonial feelings and, more generally, feelings of sympathy for the underdog. As I will point out in Chapter IX, such generous feelings are strongly based in the inherited ethos of Western civilization.

Those attitudes are not absent even in the old colonial countries in Western Europe and in the British "white" dominions which, different from the United States, have never had to fight for their national freedom. They are, naturally, somewhat more prevalent in countries from whom the colonial empires have been taken away— Germany, Italy and now more also, in the main, the Netherlands— and in the noncolonial countries in Scandinavia, though they are even there usually held back by feelings of interest solidarity with the colonial powers and, even more, by a heavy fog of opportunistic ignorance and nonconcernedness. Nevertheless, throughout all the richer countries there is usually enough of these generous attitudes to make it difficult, or even impossible, to preserve a common front against an underdeveloped country which transgresses the interests of one or several of the richer countries.

For many reasons anticolonialism and a sympathy for the poorer nations are very much stronger in the United States of America than anywhere else in the richer countries, either in Western Europe or in the "white" British dominions. In Europe and still more in the underdeveloped parts of the world I have observed that ordinary people and also politicians have no real appreciation of how important this trait in American culture is and, more particularly, how severely in practice it limits the ability of the United States government to support the old colonial powers in Western Europe who are its political allies.

The average American citizen is apt to suspect the motives of those powers in their dealings with political dependencies or former dependencies. Were it not for all the complicated tactical interests involved in carrying on a cold war by means of a great number of very diverse and often fragile alliances, the United States would even more often, and more bluntly, come out on the side of the poorer countries. In particular it would back the liberation movements in the countries which are still political dependencies.

From the viewpoint of its allies among the colonial powers, the United States actually does this often enough to cause dissatisfaction. The Dutch blamed the United States for the liberation of Indonesia. When more recently the Indonesians repudiated their financial obligations to the Netherlands, many Dutchmen again felt that the

United States carried the ultimate responsibility, as in their view a sterner line of policy in Washington toward the newly liberated countries would have prevented it. The Australians feel bitter against the Americans for having encouraged the people in West Guinea to dream of a development toward political independence and to ask for a definite timetable for its realization. And on many occasions in recent years French journalists and politicians have alternately accused the Americans and the Russians of instigating the Arabs in North Africa to rebellion.

On a still deeper level than the attitudes which are in the tradition of anticolonialism is the widespread vague consciousness in all the richer nations that the misery in the poorer countries carries an element of injustice and moral wrongfulness, and that it holds some unknown, stupendous and ominous menace to their own security. To some extent this ties the hands of the politicians in the richer countries who wish to administer reprisals against an underdeveloped country.

Relevance of the Soviet Orbit

In the Preface it was spelled out that the exposition in this book refers only to the non-Soviet world. This abstract assumption has, however, no real significance for the analysis contained in Chapters I to V. Even the liquidation of the colonial system and the absence of a world state, discussed in Chapter V, are things which have their main causes outside the Soviet orbit. Neither is the abstraction relevant for the treatment in the next chapter of certain very general problems related to economic planning. The problems of the national policies of underdeveloped countries dealt with in this chapter and, in particular, of the development of the relations between the two classes of nations in the non-Soviet world do, however, very definitely depend also upon what happens within the Soviet orbit and upon the consequences of those happenings on the political and economic relations to the rest of the world and to the underdeveloped nations in particular.

The momentous changes in both respects which after Stalin's death are taking place with an accelerating speed should, therefore, rightly be taken up at this stage of our argument. The question should be asked what significance they will have for the problems of national policies in underdeveloped countries. Therefore, if we stop our analysis at this point without attempting to answer this question, the implication is that, while in earlier chapters we could arrive at a closed system of definite conclusions, the present chapter will have to end with some huge question marks.

VII.

National Economic Planning in Underdeveloped Countries

Agreement on the Necessity of a State Plan

THE MOST important change in state policies in underdeveloped countries is the common understanding that they should each and all have a national economic development policy.

Indeed it is also universally urged that each of them should have an over-all, integrated national plan. All underdeveloped countries are now attempting to provide themselves with such a plan, except a few that have not yet been reached by the Great Awakening.

It is assumed by all that it is the state that must be responsible for both initiating the over-all plan and seeing that it is carried out. From one point of view the plan is a program for the strategy of a national government in applying a system of state interferences with the play of the market forces, thereby conditioning them in such a way as to give an upward push to the social process.

Because of the various deficiencies in a backward country it is also accepted by everybody that the government will have to take over many functions which in most advanced countries in the Western world are left to private business. In much of the contemporary literature on economic underdevelopment and development—and particularly in that larger part of it which is written in the advanced countries—the matter is sometimes confused by an altogether unfounded counterposition of central state planning and "free enterprise" and by assuming that planning creates rigidities.

It should be clear, however, that, if an underdeveloped country really succeeds in starting and sustaining by its policy interferences an upward cumulative process of economic developmnt, this will provide more and not less space for what private enterprise such a country possesses or is able to foster. And the central planning will constantly have to aim at breaking the rigidities, which are the mark of underdevelopment, and to seek to establish greater flexibility in the entire economic and social fabric.[1]

But quite apart from the question of where the line is drawn between public and private responsibility—which is usually not a question of principle but of practical expediency—the national government is expected to assume by means of the plan, and the co-ordinated system of state interferences making up the operational part of it, responsibility for the direction of the entire economic development of the country.

The emergence in the underdeveloped countries of this common urge to economic development as a major political issue and the definition of economic development as a rise in the levels of living of the common people, the agreement that economic development is a task for governments, and that governments must prepare and enforce a general economic plan, containing a system of purposefully applied controls and impulses to get development started and to keep it going—all this amounts to something entirely new in history. It represents, indeed, an attempt at a complete reversal of what once happened in the now-developed countries as described by the Schumpeterian model.

What we witness is not only how this much more than half of mankind living in poverty and distress is taking on the pursuit on a grand scale of a line of policy in which the state takes responsibility for economic development, but that positive and urgent advice to do so is given to them by all scholars and statesmen from the advanced countries and by their governments when participating in solemn resolutions of all the intergovernmental organizations. Ap-

---

[1] Cf. United Nations Economic Commission for Latin America, *Analyses and Projections of Economic Development, I.* An Introduction to the Techniques of Programming, New York, 1955, pp. 3 ff.

parently nobody in the advanced countries sees any other way out of the difficulties which are mounting in the underdeveloped countries, however different his attitude may be toward economic problems at home.

Major Problems of State Planning

A main purpose of every national development plan is to proclaim a decision to increase the total amount of investment aimed at raising the productive powers of the country and to define the means by which this can be done.

The plan must determine this over-all amount and must, in addition, determine the proportions of the capital to be allocated in different directions: to increasing the over-all facilities in transport and power production; to constructing new plants and acquiring the machinery for heavy industries and for light industries of various types; to raising the level of productivity in agriculture by long-term investments in irrigation schemes and short-term investments in tools, machinery and fertilizers; to improving the levels of health, education and training of the working people, and so on.

To be practical and effective the plan must not only be a general scheme but must have this adequately worked out in detail directives by careful planning of the different sectors. And it must spell out instructions for the specific inducements and controls by which the realization of those directives is to be effected.

The plan should learn from the industrially advanced countries that national integration toward greater social mobility and regional economic equality is conducive to rapid and sustained economic growth in the country as a whole. A main purpose of the state policies blueprinted in the plan, therefore, must be to increase the strength of the spread effects of the development impulses as among the regions and among occupations. In this respect most underdeveloped countries are up against state institutions of social and economic inequality which often cannot easily be broken. Frequently the state is itself initially in the hands of social groups which have an interest in preserving the traditional social chasms.

Breaking those social chasms and, more generally, creating a psychological, ideological, social and political situation propitious to economic development become of paramount importance. The land reforms have their significance in the national plan not only as a precondition for raising productivity in agriculture but, more primarily, as a means of shattering the foundations of the stale class structure of a stagnating society. Reforms in the field of health and education also have this double purpose of directly raising the productivity of the population and at the same time reconditioning the individuals and society so that rational motives become of greater consequence.

To help the social casualties—the sick, the maimed, the aged and, even more important, the children—will certainly be important in this general effort to strengthen the rational incentive. But it has to be done in a very economical manner. A poor underdeveloped country cannot, in the early stages of its economic development, really afford many of the redistributive measures which in the advanced countries are known under the label "social security." It should consider carefully the fact that the now highly developed countries in the early stages of their economic development had very little of it and that this type of equalizing policy came to play an important role only when the general level of average income per head had risen high above what the underdeveloped countries can hope for in any near future.

The underdeveloped country might also recall that the one-century-delayed industrial revolution which has been taking place in the Soviet Union under very different political and institutional conditions closely followed, in this one respect, the pattern of earlier capitalistic development, in that the levels of real income and consumption of the working masses were kept exceedingly low to allow for sustained rapid capital formation.

There is no other road to economic development than a forceful rise in the share of the national income which is withheld from consumption and devoted to investment. This implies a policy of the utmost austerity—quite independently of whether the increased savings are engendered by high levels of profits to be plowed back in industrial expansion or by increased taxation.

This frugality, which must be applied to the level of living of the masses of the people for the simple reason that they are the many, becomes a much more difficult policy in the underdeveloped countries today than it ever was in the now highly developed ones in their early stages of economic development. This is so both because of their much greater poverty and because of the new ideology— which had no real counterpart in the earlier history of the developed countries but has now been spread with their generous support—that the purpose of economic development is to raise levels of living for the masses of the people.

It becomes even more difficult in so far as democratic forms of government are being adopted, giving the vote to the masses. "It is not easy in some parts of the world where life is exceedingly primitive to entrust to all the people the power of democratic selection and then to ask them to forego some immediate delights. It is not easy." [2] In the advanced countries effective political suffrage was restricted by various devices to the upper-income strata until late in the development process. That type of "restricted democracy" has in our day lost its appeal.

The underdeveloped countries have to go all the way to full democracy with universal suffrage. The alternative is to remain legalized oligarchies—or, if the outer forms of democracy are adopted, to dilute those forms. But, as the inherited social stratification in these countries has been shaped by the impact of long periods of economic stagnation and is very uneven and very stale, this will in most cases imply preserving social chasms inimical to the strengthening of those centrifugal spread effects which are necessary for sustained economic development. The inequality which exists there and is preserved is not of the type to foster enterprise, savings and investments. An analogy to what once happened in the industrial revolution of the now-advanced countries is a false one.

These underdeveloped countries thus need real democracy even at this early stage in order to break down the existing impediments to economic development. But undoubtedly democracy, at the same

[2] I am again quoting from the lectures on Democratic Values by Aneurin Bevan, cited in Chapter IV.

time, makes it more difficult for governments to hold down the level of consumption in the degree necessary for rapid development. The tendency toward dynamic dictatorships of a Fascist or Communist type, visible in most parts of the underdeveloped world, should be viewed in the perspective of this basic political dilemma.

Independent of whether it is democratic, oligarchic or dictatorial, the state, which is supposed to do all this planning and put it into effect, is often in underdeveloped countries a weak state, served by a comparatively ineffective and sometimes corrupt administration. It is usually particularly weak at the provincial and local level.

Central economic planning is always a difficult thing and, where it has been tried, has seldom been a complete success in the advanced countries. Now, what amounts to a sort of superplanning has to be staged by underdeveloped countries with weak political and administrative apparatuses and largely illiterate populations.

There are reasons for expecting numerous mistakes and in many cases total failure. But the alternative to making the heroic attempt is continued acquiescence in economic and cultural stagnation, or regression, which is politically impossible in the world of today. This is, of course, the explanation why large-scale national planning is at present the goal in underdeveloped countries all over the globe and why this policy line is unanimously endorsed by the governments and experts of the advanced countries.

One more general observation: the population reproduction rate becomes of crucial importance for the national economic planning. The explosive development of medical science implies that the lowering of mortality rates, which in the now-advanced countries was a slow process stretching over generations, can be expected to happen in a very much shorter span of time in the underdeveloped countries, and that it will proceed rather independently of whether or not levels of living are, in fact, rising. In many individual parts of the underdeveloped world the death rate is already lower than it was in the advanced countries in the childhood of generations still living. There is no reason why their situation should not become the normal one in underdeveloped countries within a decade or two.

If fertility does not decrease simultaneously—and the natural effect of the health reforms is the opposite one—the rate of natural population increase will tend to rise. The underdeveloped countries today have a population about one-third larger than at the outbreak of the Second World War; they can be expected to double their population within the next thirty or forty years. In all underdeveloped countries, even in those with a fairly favorable relation between population and natural resources, a rapid increase of the population, by requiring increased investments merely in order to maintain the standard of living at present levels, will tend to hamper and slow down economic development. This implies that a given rate of development will require greater sacrifices.

The national plan should therefore include a population policy aimed at controlling fertility. A vigorous and successful birth control campaign will be needed at once to prevent the rate of natural population increase from rising.

An Induced and Controlled Cumulative Process

I shall not dwell further upon the practical difficulties to be overcome by national planning for economic development of underdeveloped countries. I have made these condensed remarks, however, in order to provide a general background to the discussion of two questions on which I should like to reflect a little more thoroughly: what, considered as an abstract model, is a national plan? and from where can it rationally derive its criteria?

The answer to the first question follows from what has been said before. A national plan should be a blueprint of a cumulative process of economic development in a country, as this process will evolve when started, sustained and controlled by certain induced exogenous changes in the social system, represented by purposeful state interferences as defined in the plan. This blueprint must therefore be built on a study of the circular causation running back and forth between all relevant factors in the social system of the country, "economic" as well as "noneconomic."

The hypothesis of circular causation, which tends to be the doctrine of despair for the poorer countries as long as they leave things to take their natural course, holds out glittering prizes for a policy of purposive interferences. Applied to a goal-directed national endeavor it promises results much bigger than the efforts—if the efforts succeed in starting a cumulative process upward.

From my account of the development problems of the American Negro people in Chapter II—which served as a concrete exemplification of the circular causation of a cumulative development process—I drew the general conclusion that, precisely because of the fact of circular causation, an upward movement can be effected by any number of policy measures, rather independently of where the initial push is applied. But I also stressed that from the point of view of economy of effort, i.e., in order to obtain a maximum upward movement of the entire system as a result of a given amount of sacrifice, it matters very much how a development problem is tackled. From this point of view the national plan is the determination of a strategy for state interferences aimed at maximizing the general economic advance of a country, given the sacrifices the people can safely be expected to accept. Because of its general poverty, an underdeveloped country is in desperate need of ascertaining through careful study the means of maximizing the effects of the efforts it can afford to put in.

I stress the need that the plan should be founded on study, and indeed study of some of the least accessible functional relationships in the social system: namely, the coefficients of circular causation between all the factors in the system. I believe that the emphasis on the need for such a study is entirely justified on rational grounds. Real progress in national planning, gradually lifting it to the plane of advanced applied social science, will come when and as our knowledge is enriched about these relationships.

At the same time it needs also to be stressed that a national plan is a strategy for action. A government committed to bring about economic development is not in a position to wait for knowledge to become as complete and certain as would be desirable. It has to make the best estimate of facts and relations it can and to decide on this basis.

Nevertheless, even from that practical point of view it is most important that the government should clearly understand the logical implications of the plan and what facts and relations are relevant to it.

Planning Must Be Done in Real Terms

My next point is this: the national plan cannot rationally be made in terms of the costs and profits of individual enterprises.

Most of the investments to be planned are not profitable from the market point of view. This is true not only of the big investments, where the main purpose is to create the external economies for industries which are not yet in existence but are planned for a distant future, perhaps on the other side of a five- or ten-year plan.

It is equally true of investment in most of the manufacturing industries. In fact, the reason why they have not been made earlier, and why they would not be made now without the incentive provided by the state in one form or another, is simply that they cannot be expected to produce the product for sale at a competitive price.

Most generally the explanation why there are unemployed and underemployed workers in an underdeveloped country is that the market provides no effective demand for their labor. Indeed, the explanation why a region or a country has a stagnating economy is that it cannot compete successfully. And from this point of view the whole meaning of a national plan is to give investment such protection from the market forces as will permit it to be undertaken in spite of the fact that it would not be remunerative according to private business calculations.

It is here that the national state comes in as representing the common and long-term interests of the community at large. It senses the inadequacy of private business calculations in terms of costs and profits as they do not reflect faithfully the social goals of national planning. From the point of view of the common long-term interests of a nation every new investment and every new enterprise has another and additional sort of yield than the expected money return to the private or public firm having made them. This is so if we can assume that the aggregate of new investments and new enterprises, provided for in the plan, can succeed in touching off a cumulative process of economic growth.

The extra-profit yields consist of the value of the external economies which almost every new enterprise bestows upon other enterprises, now or in a future which might be distant, the value of expanding markets, the value of increasing the number of trained workers and, to the extent that levels of living can gradually be raised, the productive value of higher levels of consumption in general and, in particular, of higher standards of health, education and culture. It is inherent in the circular causation within the entire economic and social fabric during a cumulative expansion process that the final results as measured in the rise of production and national income should be many times greater than the initial costs implied in getting the system under way and keeping it moving, and the extra-profit yields represent these dynamic social gains.

In the national plan these additional economic effects have to be accounted for. It is, indeed, necessary to complement the profit calculations by calculations of those other yields also—both generally in order to give a definite purpose to state interferences and, more particularly, in order to give a rational basis to the decisions of the national plan on the crucial questions of the setting of specific targets and the balancing of these various interferences. Such decisions are necessary for determining, in a scheme of rationally motivated priorities, the level of investment, the distribution of investment among different industries and between industry and agriculture as a whole, and to health, education and training schemes, and so on, and the means by which the required results have to be achieved.

None of these questions can be answered nor, indeed, can the plan be constructed in simple market terms. A whole cumulative expansion process has to be blueprinted in terms of concrete investment projects and their effects: on the volume of production in various lines, on consumption, on the employment of workers and natural resources, on health, education and the productiveness of labor, and so on, in various sectors and in different years, with main attention focused on the circular causal interactions among all the factors in the system. The plan must also determine the concrete state interferences to be applied in the markets in order to assure that the process really comes off and develops as planned.

In real life the government has, as I pointed out, to be satisfied with very approximative estimates. The point is, however, that these estimates must concern the really important things, not the largely irrelevant market phenomena.

The Price System Does Not Give Rational Criteria for Economic Planning

Naturally, the various elements of the price system—and, more specifically, money costs, prices and profit rates—constitute the terms in which in practice the national plan has largely to be spelled out. It provides a main means of detail comparisons within the plan, and most decisions from day to day on how to combine factors of production will have to be based on calculations of "opportunity costs" expressed in this manner.

In fact, a large part of the direction of the economic process toward the targets aimed at in the national plan has to be effected by changing costs, prices and profit rates through modifying the conditions under which the price system functions. To an extent this implies the transference of the social extra-profit yields into individual profits: in the ideal case the modification of the price system would have absorbed them altogether, so that individual profit rates gave motivations perfectly harmonious with the goals of the national plan.

The criteria for the national planning are, however, entirely outside the price system. There do not exist any "objective" criteria for economic planning. The plan and its targets have in the final analysis to be determined by decisions which represent choices made among different, alternatively possible, sets of goals and means. These choices are policy decisions, reached in terms of national development goals as determined by the political process.

From the beginning of the twenties there was a lively discussion in our learned journals about the possibility of any rationality in a planned economy. It was started off by Professor Ludvig von Mises, who declared that economic planning must fail, because the absence of a free market and of a cost and profit system untampered with by the state would preclude the application of any economic criteria to determine in an objective way what should or should not be done.

This thought, that there are such things as "objective" criteria for determining how the social process should evolve and that the market itself provides these objective criteria while planning is necessarily "arbitrary," contains in a nutshell all the inherited, irrational predilections holding back economic theory which I refer to in Part Two.

The ironical fact is that this very type of economic planning, the rationality of which was so recently explained to be an impossibility on logical grounds, is now proceeding in almost all underdeveloped countries—often with the competent guidance of economists, many of whom, in another compartment of their thinking, harbor whole learned structures of fallacious arguments in the old tradition to which von Mises did no more than give a particularly unqualified, and therefore crude, expression.[3]

The price system as a part of a very irrational whole, namely, the economy of a backward and stagnating country, can hardly have any great claim on rationality to begin with. It could even less form the rational basis for those "economic" and "objective" criteria as, furthermore, its continuous modification is a necessary part of the state interferences which form the operative part of the national plan. In the ideal case the price system would have been modified so as to give a faithful expression to the goals of the national plan, which is, however, almost the contrary to itself providing the criteria for determining those modifications.

[3] Many Socialist writers have fallen in line with the main assumptions of von Mises' argument but have taken the opposite stand and insisted that it is quite possible for economic planning to be rational by maximizing "welfare."

The modern dispute is very much only a restaging of very old controversies. Among others, Gustav Cassel presented his version of the liberalistic doctrine more than fifty years ago. And all the important elements in the modern Socialist welfare doctrine can still earlier be found in a book by von Wieser—who was not a Socialist—on the Natural Value which, according to him, would be realized in the "perfect Communist state" (*Der natürliche Wert*, Vienna, 1889).

As I noted at the end of Chapter IV, we have, by a long and gradual process of public and private organization of the markets, in our industrial and highly integrated countries succeeded fairly well, on the whole, in making the price system our servant and not our master—though, curiously enough, this is usually not fully recognized in popular debate. In many of the most thoroughly organized economies, like those of Switzerland and the United States, this debate is often carried on as if prices were actually set by the laws of supply and demand under free competition between "free enterprises," which is very far from the truth.

The underdeveloped countries are now embarking on this difficult task of assuming control over the price system and conditioning it to operate as an effective means of carrying out their national plans. And they are pressed by circumstances to do it in a much more sudden and complete way and on a much weaker political and administrative basis.

Not a Gospel of License

When stressing the fact that a national economic plan cannot be rationally constructed by the application of the criteria of the price system and private business profitability but that the plan must consist of the blueprinting in real terms of a cumulative process of circular causation, in the final analysis directed by political decisions, I am not preaching a gospel of license—quite the contrary.

To reach deeper than the registration of the market phenomena and to ascertain the intricate causal interrelations as they would operate in a planned cumulative development process is an analytical task of supreme difficulty. If I am right, however, there is no other way to rational economic planning than to attempt calculations of these interrelations in real terms and not as they are distorted by represented prices, costs and profits. If practical planning, at least for a long time, has to be founded on very approximate estimates of extra-profit yields, the estimates have nevertheless to concern these much less accessible economic and social phenomena.

This approach, if effectively carried out, will in the practical sphere spell out reasons for an economic policy of suppressing the temptations to raise levels of living rapidly. A poor underdeveloped country which, in the difficult circumstances I have hinted at in the beginning of this chapter, has the ambition to "lift itself by its own bootstraps" and start on a sustained economic development process must, indeed, count inputs and outputs in the most careful manner and generally apply a policy of frugality.

Indeed, a major purpose of the national plan is to effect the strictest economy with the available resources. Rational economic behavior is always concerned with allocating scarce resources among alternative uses; this is the reality behind the notion of "opportunity costs." If, as a matter of fact, many underdeveloped countries demonstrate a shocking waste of very scarce resources in "showpiece" public works and in subsidizing expensive starts of investment and production along blind alleys, this is the result of a failure in planning, and the only cure is to improve the planning. This involves getting down to a realistic analysis of the concrete circular causal relations involved in the cumulative development process.

Another purpose of the plan is to overcome the rigidities which characterize an underdeveloped economy. The strategy of economic planning in underdeveloped countries must very largely consist in foreseeing by rational analysis where the bottlenecks due to particularly tough rigidities are likely to arise and then to direct policy measures accordingly. Rational economic planning must aim at enlarging markets and utilizing for its purposes the price formation that takes place in the markets which are thus expanded. This is, however, not at all the same thing as taking the criteria for the planning itself from these market phenomena which are its own creation or results of its modifications.

A third general purpose of national economic planning is to free the minds of the people and the governments from many popular preconceptions, often originating from their envious comparisons with the highly developed countries, which otherwise are certain to dominate the economic policies in underdeveloped countries. The only way to do this is by knowledge of the true causal relationships as revealed by rational planning in real terms.

International Trade under National Economic Planning

These principles apply equally, of course, to international trade. The development plan of an underdeveloped country will as a rule require large purchases of capital equipment from abroad. If, as is usually the case, this increase in imports is not fully covered by gifts or loans from outside, the underdeveloped country will have to do its utmost to increase its exports. Its ability to do this, however, will be limited both by its own productive facilities and often by the inelastic nature of the foreign demand; and it may also have to restrict its imports of consumption goods, and of luxury goods in particular, if it is to obtain the essential imports it requires.

These induced changes in the composition of its foreign trade will have to be matched by production increases in agriculture and manufacturing industries to stop inflation, and also by price and consumption regulations at home in order to prevent the demand for luxury imports from providing incentives for an undesirable direction of investments and production at home. The capital formation for raising the level of investment has at the same time to be matched by higher savings procured by various policy measures. All these induced changes in the quantities of consumption, production, exports and imports are essential elements in the national plan.

As investment and production are going up and as factors of production then have to be induced to move into new combinations, some internal inflationary pressure must always be expected in a country which is embarking upon economic development. Even if this is carefully controlled, the process of development is likely to be reflected in higher money incomes and demand for consumption goods; and some of the increased demand will always turn toward imports. As in any case the increased imports of capital goods are bound to put pressure on the exchange resources, an underdeveloped country bent upon economic development will be compelled to apply import restrictions in order to protect its exchange balance, quite apart from any other reasons.

These import restrictions, which thus under all conditions become necessary even without any designs for protection, fit into the national plan which, as I have already pointed out, assumes that a number of investments will be made which are not competitive and therefore need shelter. As these starts of production mature to the stage where they can deliver more goods to the market they will gradually relieve the inflationary pressure and the exchange difficulties.

Some of this increased supply will have to consist in more export goods; an underdeveloped country will often even have rational reasons for subsidizing its exports in certain directions. In the actual situation of a deeply lopsided economy, which most underdeveloped countries inherit from stagnation and economic colonialism, the larger part of the production increase will be more and new goods for the home market, replacing imports and gradually allowing an increase of consumption in a more self-sufficient economy.

I am here reproducing in very much simplified form the essential elements of any national plan as observed from the angle of foreign trade and exchange. The advice underdeveloped countries are now often gratuitously given, to abstain from interfering with foreign trade and from tampering with the foreign exchanges, is in most cases tantamount to recommending them not to bother about economic development.

The advice they would really need is, instead, on how to carry into effect their trade and payments regulations and how to retain that necessary minimum of control over internal inflationary pressure which is a precondition for rational and efficient management of trade and payments regulations. This latter advice they need very badly indeed, for monetary, trade and payments policies are all fields in which an inefficient administration can make a real mess of national planning for economic development, as many sad examples demonstrate.

Special Needs for Protection

Returning to the trade regulations and their employment for protective purposes, I would insist that quite obviously they cannot be rationally framed by reference to the "objective" economic criteria of the price system, i.e., by means of a simple application of the static theory of comparative costs. Many manufacturing industries are thwarted in their growth or prevented from ever coming into existence because of the small size of the domestic market. This market is frequently flooded by foreign imports from sources to which this demand is often only marginal. By providing protection against outside competition the local industries can be given their chance.

Another general reason for protection is the fact that, as I have already pointed out, almost every new industrial enterprise yields benefits for the economy as a whole, which are not reflected in the profit calculations, in the form of external economies of all sorts, an increase in the number of trained workers, and so on. These effects are for various reasons relatively much more important in an underdeveloped country than in a developed one.

An underdeveloped country is also characterized by the fact that a large portion of its working force is unemployed or eking out a bare subsistence through various forms of "disguised unemployment." This fact that labor is not productively employed is from one point of view a way of stating that the country is underdeveloped; from another point of view it represents its opportunity to become developed. If part of this "free" labor can become gainfully employed, it is a net advantage for the country even if, for this purpose, a shelter against competition needs to be erected.

In an underdeveloped country the span between wages in manufacturing industry and in agriculture tends, furthermore, for many reasons, to be particularly broad. This will hamper industry if it is not given protection to a corresponding degree.

Interferences in international trade, motivated by considerations of these types, are only part of the general efforts, defined in the national plan, to recondition the price system in such a way that a sustained cumulative process toward economic development is engendered. The action part of a national plan consists of nothing else than a system of interferences with the price system, which must be judged in terms of the practical contribution which they make toward the cumulative upward process which is the goal of the plan.

Again No Invitation to License

As applied to the field of international trade, this is again not an invitation to license.

It implies only a change of the normative standard of political judgment from the logically untenable and, indeed, fallacious doctrine of free trade, or some of its euphemisms, to the true interests and real causal relationships as they exist in an underdeveloped country and become revealed by the study of the relevant facts which the national plan should be based on.

No underdeveloped country can afford not to take most careful account of the international prices of its possible exports and imports. The prices abroad are independent variables in the problem: they are given realities which an underdeveloped country can usually not influence and modify as it can its domestic price structure.

There are, as I pointed out, sound reasons why it may choose to produce at home things which it could import more cheaply or to export things at a loss to be covered by subsidy. But those reasons must take full account of international prices as independently determined facts; if this is not done, the development process will be slowed down. The fact that protectionism can be proved to be rational in an underdeveloped country should not, of course, be used to conceal the other fact, that the interferences with international trade, as today actually applied, are grossly irrational in perhaps most underdeveloped countries.

As a matter of fact, that old chapter in the theory of international trade to which from Ricardo's time onward we have given the title "Comparative Costs" or "Comparative Advantage" is well worth preserving in the theory of economic underdevelopment and development of which we are in need. The extra-profit yields which I have referred to can be introduced into the scheme, as well as the inflationary pressures and exchange difficulties which are normal consequences of a policy of economic development. If these and some other amendments were made in a systematic way, unbiased by the inherited predilections of economic theory, what would emerge would be a dynamic theory of comparative costs, forming an integral part of the general theory of state economic planning which we need to construct.

These countries are for many reasons in a different position from that of the highly developed countries and, as I have explained in more detail in another connection, there are good reasons for a "double standard morality" so far as international trade is concerned. Much of the activity in the International Monetary Fund and in GATT and much of the bilateral negotiation about trade policy outside these organizations have been based on the principle *do ut des*. This may be appropriate in the relations between highly developed countries, but it implies a false assumption of equality so far as underdeveloped countries are concerned.

Inflationary pressure and pressure on the foreign exchange resources of underdeveloped countries are normal consequences of their economic development policy. A tight regulation of their foreign trade becomes for this reason a necessity, if they are not to give up their development policy. In addition they have, by the very facts that their economies are lopsided as a result of underdevelopment and that they lack competitive strength, special reasons, which are not present for developed countries, to use these regulations for protection. And as they will be anxious to use every opportunity to increase their imports, their regulations will not generally decrease world trade, as those of a developed country actually do if it manages to keep out of exchange difficulties.

The underdeveloped countries have rational grounds for asking the developed countries to liberalize their trade unilaterally. They need to be stanch free traders, and even preserve for themselves the right to give export subsidies, so far as the advanced countries' imports from them are concerned, but restrictionists in respect of their own imports. And they have valid arguments against anyone who would call this attitude logically inconsistent.

VIII.

A Challenge

The Underdeveloped Countries' Need of Research

IN THEIR drive for economic development the underdeveloped countries are up against much greater difficulties than the now-developed countries ever faced.

The economic level at which they start is in most cases very much lower. The relationship between population and resources is usually much more unfavorable and the population trends more dynamic and dangerous. They do not have at their disposal an international capital market as the now-developed countries had in their time, nor the outlets for emigration. They have not inherited the traditions of rationality and the rule of law which were so important in the earlier history of the now-developed countries.

And they are late-comers: they have not the opportunity, as the now-developed countries had, to advance as industrial islands in a surrounding world of backward nations which they could exploit as markets for manufactured goods and as sources of raw materials and for this purpose even keep in colonial bondage.

The one advantage they have is our accumulated scientific and technical knowledge. But to utilize this knowledge they need fresh research in all fields.

Neither our techniques of politics, administration and social reforms nor our techniques in production and distribution can with advantage be simply taken over. These techniques have been developed to suit the very different conditions of the advanced countries and are inappropriate to the needs of the underdeveloped countries.

Ideally the underdeveloped countries should utilize all the available knowledge but work out their own specific techniques to fit their values and their actual conditions. And to do this effectively they would need to carry out research on all levels, including fundamental research.

In the main, this cannot be done for them. To have any real chance to be successful in economic development the underdeveloped countries must give the highest priority to the provision of schools and universities for training scientists and conducting scientific research in all fields. I have in another connection suggested that the richer countries should consider giving really substantial aid to the foundation of such institutions. Such aid would have great and sustained effects in helping the underdeveloped countries to gather momentum in a cumulative process of development.

The Need for New Approaches in Economic Theory

The underdeveloped countries have also, for their own free use, our inherited economic theory. But, again, they should not accept this theory uncritically but remold it to fit their problems and their interests.

They should, in particular, be aware of the fact, which I take up in Part II, that much of this theory is a rationalization of the dominant interests in the industrial countries where it was first put forward and later developed. In the main, economic theory has not concerned itself with the problems of underdeveloped countries. If nevertheless it is uncritically applied to these problems, the theory becomes wrong.

As we shall see, this is quite clearly the situation as regards the theory of international trade. This theory would, indeed, suggest that trade starts a movement toward income equalization, while instead a quite normal result of unhampered trade between two countries, of which one is industrialized and the other underdeveloped, is the initiation of a cumulative process toward the impoverishment and stagnation of the latter.

Much of the advice in trade and payments matters which is currently given to underdeveloped countries has the same weak foundation in a theory which is not relevant to the problems of those countries. This means that this advice is scientifically unfounded and in practice misleading.

Most of the literature on the development problems of underdeveloped countries is even today produced in the industrially advanced countries. Fortunately it is, on the whole, rather untheoretical in its approach, which is an advantage as long as economic theory is not better adapted to those problems.

But we can also note that a large part of this literature does not take its starting point from the interests of the underdeveloped countries themselves but, consciously or unconsciously, views their problems from the national political interests of one of the advanced countries or a group of them. This situation has become much worse under the impact of the cold war, when often those national interests steering the analysis have been narrowed down to mere strategic interests in that world conflict.

As the underdeveloped nations now increasingly become articulate about their desires and worries, a change of direction of research can be expected. Economic problems will increasingly be studied from the viewpoint of their interests. As this is also the viewpoint of the equality ideal, which has always had such a basic position in economic theory, this new direction of economic research will be very much in line with strong and deep urges in our Western civilization, which stem from the age of Enlightenment and even from still further back.

It is my view, for which I attempt to give the reasons in this book, that this new orientation of economic theory toward greater realism in regard to existing economic inequalities will imply the final liquidation of the old laissez-faire predilections and, more specifically, the free trade doctrine and the stable equilibrium approach. Also, the distinction between "economic factors" and "noneconomic factors" will likewise have to be discarded as illogical and, consequently, misleading. Economic analysis will have to deal with all the relevant factors if it wants to be realistic; general economic theory will have to become social theory.

I believe that the main hypothesis for this new theory will be the assumption of circular causation among all factors in the social system resulting in a cumulative process, and I have tried to sketch an outline of a general theory of this kind. The outline hardly gives more than a vision of what has to be accomplished before we can really talk about a general theory for the economic process. In this new theory there would be place for many special arguments and theories which are now included in our inherited theory. They would thus be salvaged for continued use in a new setting; to this point I will revert in Chapter XI.

Let me add also that I have no great illusions that it will ever be possible to fit such a general theory into a neat econometric model. The relevant variables and the relevant relations between them are too many to permit that sort of heroic simplification. This does not mean, however, that particular problems could not with great advantage be treated in this way—provided the variables and assumptions were selected on the basis of such insight into what the essential facts and relations are as only a general theory can furnish.

I feel sure that in the years to come economists in all countries will increasingly come to study the development problems of under-developed countries in the light of the interests, values and aspirations of those countries themselves. But, undoubtedly, the primary responsibility rests upon their own young economists. When lecturing in Cairo, the capital of one of the poorest and most restive of the underdeveloped countries, it was natural to me that at the end I addressed myself to the many students in my audience and spelled out to them what I consider to be a great challenge and an opportunity. And even if this volume seeks a wider audience, I find it appropriate that I should give a summary record here of what I then said.

The Role of the Young Economists in the Underdeveloped Countries

In this epoch of the Great Awakening it would be pathetic if the young economists in the underdeveloped countries got caught in the predilections of the economic thinking in the advanced countries, which are hampering the scholars there in their efforts to be rational but would be almost deadening to the intellectual strivings of those in the underdeveloped countries.

I would, instead, wish them to have the courage to throw away large structures of meaningless, irrelevant and sometimes blatantly inadequate doctrines and theoretical approaches and to start their thinking afresh from a study of their own needs and problems. This would then take them far beyond the realm of both outmoded Western liberal economics and Marxism.

Instead of chewing over our old doctrines and doctrinal controversies, many of them a hundred years old or more, they should take their pick of what is really practical and useful in our tradition and then proceed to make their own theoretical constructions to suit their problems. They would then find that many old and familiar arguments and theorems became useful when adjusted to fit into a new frame.

All the underdeveloped countries are now starting out on a line of economic policy which has no close historical precedent in any advanced country. In the same way as the course of economic events and policies in those advanced countries always gave rise to new realignments of social and economic theories better fitted to, and closely conditioned by, the immediate historical circumstances, it would be entirely appropriate if the very different events and policies in the underdeveloped countries today were accepted as a challenge to produce new and different theoretical frames for social and economic research.

If this hope could come true, an incidental effect of the awakening of this large majority of mankind, which has up till now mainly subsisted in economic and cultural backwardness, would be new scientific discoveries and the widening of our spiritual horizon—in the end the enrichment of our common culture. It is under the inspiration of this brave hope that in this volume, as earlier in the lectures upon which it is based, I permit myself to deal in somewhat provocative terms with a number of the inherited theoretical approaches as they have been fashioned in the privileged countries during their period of economic advance and unchallenged intellectual hegemony over the world.

In one respect the students from underdeveloped countries should have an initial special advantage: namely, that normally they should be further detached from the particular needs for rationalization that have dominated the development of economic theory in the relatively rich and advanced countries. It is, indeed, natural that they take as their starting point the need to satisfy the demands of the destitute masses in the underdeveloped countries. With them the tendency would thus rather be that the equality doctrine came to serve as the antidote to the conservative laissez-faire predilections instead of vice versa in our Western tradition (Chapter X).

In the process of transmittal of economic theory to the great and growing number of students in the underdeveloped countries, I see the chance for an even more fundamental change than the one from the predominance of one type of doctrinal predilections to that of another one. For in freeing themselves from the earlier type of predilections they naturally get involved in a logical criticism of them and the theory that harbored them. As they thus are brought to take a viewpoint placed outside the doctrinal tradition in economics, there then exists the possibility that they might come to see for themselves how these predilections represent a metaphysical and teleological element in our thinking: the old artifice of treating values as facts.

And they might rise to the ambition of avoiding altogether this irrational element in their thinking. The chance that they may do so is admittedly slight. As the history of social sciences demonstrates, the normal and natural thing would be that they speedily equip themselves with new predilections of their own, corresponding to their different rationalization needs, and fortify these predilections by building them into a new metaphysical system. But it should not be excluded that some of them might attempt to use the transitional moment of intellectual freedom, when they are in the course of liberating themselves from our doctrinal predilections, consciously to start out with the intention of constructing a social theory free from objectified valuations.

The rational way to do this is to work with explicit value premises, not only when drawing the practical and political inferences but, prior to that, when ascertaining and analyzing the facts and the causal relations. This methodological clarification and its application in their scientific work would sharpen their analytical tools and make these tools much more powerful also when used for practical and political purposes.

To pick out what is really useful and practical in our traditional theoretical approaches—to throw away the ballast but at the same time shape what is of value in the old arguments and theorems so as to fit into a different approach to economic and social problems—is, however, by no means an easy accomplishment. It is not a task for dilettanti and ignorance—they are usually the first to succumb to traditional predilections or some of their popular perversions, often without even realizing their intellectual bondage.

They are the least original. No critic has ever been effective without knowing thoroughly what he was criticizing. The steeply climbing path I am sketching out for the young social scientists in the underdeveloped countries demands, in fact, the most intense efforts to attain to true learning and the fullest mastery of the entire theoretical heritage.

It is much easier to be a conformist than a competent rebel.

Part Two

Economic Inequalities, the Public Conscience and Economic Theory

IX.

The Equality Doctrine and the Escape
from It

IN THE first chapter of this book I pointed out that our inherited body of economic theory has been very little concerned with the important facts of the existing inequalities as between countries and between regions within a country. The rest of this book will be devoted to an attempt to explain why this has been so. These inequalities form, of course, only one aspect of the wider problem of the inequalities generally as between individuals and social groups in society.

The Radical Tenets of Western Civilization

All in the small group of the richer nations are now effective democracies, and all have embarked, though only in recent decades, on far-reaching policies to diminish economic inequalities between regions and social classes within their own boundaries. There are important relations between economic development, political democracy and economic equalization policies, which I discussed in Chapter IV.

At this point in the argument, however, I want to stress the fact that from the beginning, indeed long before these countries were in any true sense political democracies or had undertaken any of the modern equalization policies, the economic and social theories prevalent there were strongly egalitarian. These theories had at their very roots ultraradical policy premises, directly emanating from the

philosophies which had developed in the general cultural setting of
what we call Western civilization.[1]

From the philosophy of natural law emerged the doctrine of
labor's moral superiority as title to property: labor was the only
"creator of wealth." In its modern formulation this idea stems from
Locke; it materialized in the classical theory of "real value" which
assumed labor as the only real "factor of production."[2]

From the natural law philosophy came also the idea that "all men
are born equal." Primarily this doctrine was understood in a moral
sense that all have the same rights in society. This was conceived as
an evident truth, needing no other support than unbiased reflection
over the social relations in natural society where those relations were
not distorted by unnatural and unjustified institutions. It would
hold true even if natural endowments were dissimilar. That a man
was less gifted should not infringe upon his rights.

But the moralistic doctrine of equality of rights undoubtedly
gathered additional strength by the naturalistic doctrine, which from
Locke onward was also prominently placed in natural law philosophy, minimizing the individual differences as to innate qualities
and aptitudes. To Locke, the spiritual father of French as well as
English Enlightenment philosophy, the newborn child was a *tabula
rasa* upon which the "sensations"—that is, in modern language, the
entirety of life experiences—later made their imprint. Environment
was thus made supreme, and, this was the basis of the rationalistic
optimism of the age.

When later individual variations in natural endowments were increasingly recognized, the theory was nevertheless upheld for comparisons between groups of people. As we know, modern research
has in the past half century gone a long way to prove scientifically

[1] For what follows in Part II, see the author's *The Political Element in the
Development of Economic Theory*, Routledge and Kegan Paul, London,
1953; see also "The Relation between Social Theory and Social Policy,"
The British Journal of Sociology, September, 1953, pp. 211 ff., and a forthcoming volume: *Value in Social Theory. A Selection of Essays on Methodology*, by Gunnar Myrdal, edited by Paul Sheeten, Routledge and Kegan
Paul, London, 1957.

[2] *The Political Element in the Development of Economic Theory*, pp. 64 ff.

the correctness of this essential kernel of the naturalistic doctrine of equality with respect to natural endowments and thereby justified the environmental approach in the social sciences which gives strength to rational radicalism in social reform.

At this stage of our exposition the point to stress is, however, simply that the naturalistic equality doctrine, though it fortified the moralistic one, is not a logically necessary premise for it; nor can the moralistic doctrine be logically inferred from the naturalistic one. When in this volume I refer to the equality doctrine, it is the moralistic thesis of all men's equal rights that I have in mind.

The utilitarian philosophers in their turn developed further the old concept of a "general welfare." They took over from the natural law philosophy its implicit hedonistic psychology and elaborated it with the intention of providing the empirical basis for the calculation of "pleasures" and "pains," the arithmetical sum of which was supposed to constitute the "general welfare." The main thesis of utilitarianism was that it was the rational policy goal of organized society that this sum should be maximized. In the philosophical tradition through generations, out of which economic theory branched off, it was never disputed, and is not disputed today, that in the calculation of the "general welfare" every individual human being should be counted as equal to every other individual.

From the hedonistic psychology was also derived the idea of the diminishing "marginal utility" of an income unit as the total income increased. It was early accepted, and only further elaborated by Bentham and James Mill, that this idea provided a general proof for the principle that equalization of wealth and incomes was in the interest of society.

As the expression of an ideal the equality doctrine may have the full support of our sentiment in that we find it corresponds to our desire of how things ought to be in the world—and the author may be permitted to state his complete allegiance to this general valuation, basic to the moral ambitions of Western civilization. In the present study the ideal of equality of opportunity is posited as one of the two main value premises, the other being the desirability of political democracy. But judged as "theory" where, in the fashion just illustrated, the ideal is "proved" to be a logical inference from premises of facts this is all a lot of empty metaphysics with no relation to reality.

These various currents of the ultraradical equality ideal—"proved" in so many different ways and given a slightly different logical content depending upon its particular theoretical derivation—came together during the Enlightenment period and formed from then on a main element of the political conscience of the Western world. But the sources of these streams have to be sought much further back in mankind's history. All great religions and philosophies have, on a general plane, been egalitarian. It is a still largely unsolved sociological problem why and how it happened that this shining idealistic vision of the dignity of the individual human being and of his basic right to equality of opportunity originated and maintained its strength through untold centuries of blatant inequality and oppression.

The concepts and arguments applied in performing the "proofs" of the equality doctrine and giving it a pretended logical justification came to form the foundation stones of the classical economic theory which was built up during the Enlightenment period and gradually perfected in the first half of the nineteenth century. In the Preface to his *Lectures on Political Economy,* Knut Wicksell points this out:

> As soon as we begin seriously to regard economic phenomena *as a whole* and to seek for the conditions of the welfare of the whole, considerations for the interests of the proletariat must emerge; and from thence to the proclamation of *equal* rights for all is only a short step. The very concept of political economy, therefore, or the existence of a science with such a name implies, strictly speaking, a thoroughly revolutionary programme.[3]

The equality doctrine had thus fastened itself at the rock bottom of Western economic speculation. On a very general level it thereafter represented, and represents today, a link between the philosophies of Conservative and Radicals, Liberals and Socialists. It

[3] Quoted from the English translation, *Lectures on Political Economy,* Vol. I., "General Theory," Routledge Sons, London, 1934, p. 4.

determines the way in which they commonly present and justify their strivings.

This is related to the fact that modern economic speculation has never really gone outside the forms in which it was originally set: the philosophies of natural law and of utilitarianism and the psychology implied in these philosophies of hedonism.[4] This can be verified, for instance, by a careful analysis of the implicit assumptions of any of our most recently published textbooks on economic theory.

An Ideological Force

As I have already hinted, the equality doctrine is not merely an abstract formula propounded in books and speeches. It is also an expression of a living ideal and as such part of social reality: a valuation, actually perceived by people to be morally right. This is an important political fact. Thanks to this, the equality doctrine or, rather, the ideal it expresses became an ideological force in society, influencing—in some measure—human strivings. Over the ages it has always pulled in one direction: toward greater equality of economic opportunity.

This long ideological pull must not be forgotten when explaining the more recent development in the richer countries toward national integration and an ever-fuller realization of equality of opportunity. The Great Awakening in the very poor countries, which is now under way, also reflects, of course, the equality ideal of Western civilization. From one point of view its essence is, indeed, that this

[4] The natural law arguments lead to the demand for equality of opportunities; if natural endowments were not the same, this would still leave certain inequalities in incomes and wealth in existence. In principle, hedonistic utilitarianism goes further and demands equality of income and wealth (later utilitarians as, for instance, Edgeworth complicated the scheme by taking into consideration also the inborn capacities to enjoy happiness, which might not be equal for all men). As every society is very far away from a state of equality, however defined, this logical difference is of no great importance. The practical demand raised by the equality doctrine is always for social reform which would change society in the direction of greater equality. The natural law ideal of equality of opportunity has *a fortiori* utilitarian support.

old inherited ideal of the richer countries is now rapidly and effectively being spread in the underdeveloped world and is there spur-
ring the peoples into revolt against their poverty—with a very
apparent implication that their poverty is not all their fault.

This radical equality doctrine, underlying the basic philosophies
and also reflected in people's actual attitudes, has for centuries been
something of an anomaly in a world characterized by gross inequalities and mainly ruled by vested interests bent upon preserving
those inequalities. Let me stress again that the surprising thing is not
that our society has all the time tolerated so much economic inequality but that through the ages people have kept a sanctuary in
their minds for such a high-pitched ideal as is expressed by the
equality doctrine.

Even within each of the Western countries there has been all the
time a great disparity between, on the one hand, social reality, including everyday human behavior, and, on the other hand, this
radical equality doctrine continuously upheld *in abstracto*. Indeed,
in the period around the end of the eighteenth and the beginning of
the nineteenth century, when in the literature of the advanced countries the equality doctrine was spelled out most explicitly and given
particularly great emphasis, the economic inequalities in those countries as between regions and social classes were appalling.

At that time very little was done by way of reform policies, directed toward mitigating the inequalities. The policies then actually
propounded by the economists were usually not very radical, viewed
in the light of what has later been accomplished in those countries.
They were, of course, still less radical in the light of the equality
doctrine which held such a dominant position in literature and
public debate in this period.

The Belief in Innate Differences

This moral situation can only be fully understood if we realize
that in a queer coexistence with the radical equality doctrine there
persisted also the age-old reactionary belief in innate differences in
quality between groups of people having different standards of
economic well-being. I have already stressed that in pure logic the

moralistic equality doctrine that men have equal rights is not dependent on a premise that men are equally endowed by nature. But certainly it is easier to adhere to the first ideal, and to give it practical expression in social reform, if the latter proposition is also accepted as true.

All discussion of social reform turns very much, in the final instance, on the vexed problem of the relative importance of nurture and nature. A Swedish political scientist of the generation which has now passed, Rudolf Kjellen, once ventured the observation that the radical is inclined to believe that the occasion makes the thief, while the conservative rather suspects that the thief is likely to find the occasion. According to the radical, the blame and the responsibility for what is imperfect in society are placed on the environment, which can be changed. The individual, and thereby also society, can be improved by social reform.

The conservative, on the contrary, is apt to think that it is human nature and not environment which, on the whole, makes individuals and society what they are. Human nature is unchangeable. This is a reason and a justification for the conservative's skepticism in regard to social reform. He is therefore inclined toward a policy of *laissez faire* or do nothing.

As I pointed out, the philosophies of the Enlightenment period, which formed the basis for economic theory, depreciated differences in human nature. Man and society could be reformed by altering the social institutions. But the belief in innate differences, not only between individuals but between groups, also persisted. In one particular respect the secularist rationalism of the Enlightenment, by placing *homo sapiens* in the natural order as an animal, even gave increased emphasis to human nature and made it more likely on *a priori* grounds that there could be distinct species of men. It was first in the eighteenth century that the word and concept "race" was born, opening up, for example, the possibility of defending the holding of Negroes in slavery by arguments of social inferiority instead of the old theological justification that they were pagans. Later Darwin's theory of the survival of the fittest gave a rationalizing explanation why differences in qualities should be expected as the result of evolution.

On the whole, however, the social sciences and, in particular, economic theory stuck stubbornly to the naturalistic equality postulate that as a general rule all men were equally endowed by nature; they could thereby also uphold the environmental approach. And, as I noted, the research in recent decades on group differentials of intelligence and other mental capacities and aptitudes has given this fundamental presumption of social and economic theories an ever-firmer scientific foundation.

The contrary belief in great and systematic differences between groups of people continued, however, to live its very real life in the convictions of ordinary people—and often also in those of the philosophers and theorists when they were away from their doctoral pursuits. This belief was never restricted to different races but was applied also to social classes within one country. Indeed, as I have just pointed out, the modern intense interest in racial differences is only a couple of centuries old, while economic, social and religious distinctions have always been important in the public mind. The poor as a class were supposed to be less well endowed intellectually and morally.

And people based their conviction on what they conceived of as their experience and on everyday observations from which they drew inferences. As a matter of fact, of course, the differences among various social strata were great, much greater than is the case today—in health, education and training, customs, morals and general culture—and these differences were reflected also in differences of productive capacities.

The philosophers and economists had a general argument to counter the inferences drawn from such observations, namely, that these differences were themselves only the result of earlier economic inequalities. But it was difficult for ordinary people to believe that this was the whole explanation. And it is apparent that even the scholars preserved a lingering doubt—and sometimes more than a doubt—that at bottom some differences were innate.

Escapism in Economic Theory

Returning to the realm of economic theory, we face a strange paradox. On the one hand, economic theory was that branch of social speculation in which the ultraradical equality doctrine was "proved" and logically sharpened into a particularly clear and cutting instrument of "objective" valuation. On the other hand, having firmly placed the equality doctrine at its structural foundation, economic theory demonstrated from the beginning a particularly strong tendency to escape from raising the equality issue.

The equality doctrine, after it had been proved, was most often confined to general statements in an abstract compartment in the basement, insulated by impregnable abstruseness—while, for the rest, economic theory was developed so as to avoid as much as possible stating problems in such a way that the equality doctrine could be used as a premise for practical policy interferences.

From John Stuart Mill on, a main device for effecting this evasion has been, as we know, the drawing of a sharp dividing line between the sphere of production, including exchange, and the sphere of distribution. In the sphere of production natural laws reigned, and policy interferences would only hamper production; distribution of incomes and wealth, on the other hand, was the sphere for policy where the equality doctrine had its legitimate space of validity.

Though this was not logically implied, and though it was not Mill's intention, economists have since then and for more than a hundred years utilized this device for the purpose of directing their analysis almost entirely on production and exchange, while expressing a general reservation in regard to distribution of incomes and wealth and the need for redistributional reform.

It is, of course, possible to explain this tendency in the direction of economic analysis by saying that the economists have in the main been interested in problems other than those pertaining to equality and inequality. They have been interested in production and in trade. In the pursuit of free science the direction of research should be left to the play of the scientific curiosity of the individual scientists, and I am the last to query this fundamental principle of academic freedom. But I maintain that the distinction between a production sphere and a distribution sphere, utilized in economic analysis for concentrating attention on the problems of production, is logically untenable;[5] and this is, from one point of view, a main explanation why many of our theories have been defective.

More fundamentally, and apart from this, it remains to be explained why, as the aggregate outcome of the inclinations of so many generations of economists, economics as a science got this particular direction of interest and so avoided, in the main, the problems of the distribution of incomes and wealth.

The Significance of Malthus

In his time Ricardo did not seek to avoid the problem of distribution. On the contrary, he proclaimed as the primary task of political economy to explain the prices of the three productive factors, labor, capital and land, and thus the distribution of income. And he stressed—and overstressed) by the static abstraction from changes and the interrelations between the changes—the interest conflict among the different economic classes: none of them could have an increased share of the social product except at the expense of one or both of the other classes.

It would seem that on the basis of this theory combined with the philosophical premises of utilitarianism, to which he firmly adhered, Ricardo should have come out for redistributional reforms on a large scale—as, indeed, many radical writers did in his own time and later, often basing their thinking on his theory of income distribution. Ricardo himself, however, and after him the writers who came to represent the classical line in economic theory stuck, on the whole, to *laissez faire* even in regard to income distribution.

This has to be related to Ricardo's theory of natural wages. This theory, in its turn, was derived from Malthus' law of population. The thought is much older, though Malthus first gave it elaboration and emphasis. In Europe its spread and influence in the beginning

[5] *Ibid.*, pp. 116, 119. *The Political Element in the Development of Economic Theory*, pp. 129 ff.

of the nineteenth century were part of the general movement toward strengthening the foundations for economic conservatism which developed in reaction to the French and American revolutions.[6]

Malthus and Ricardo did not fail to point out that ambitions for higher living standards, say as a result of better education, could alter the whole situation. But in most of their theoretical arguments they used what they took to be an empirically verified assumption, viz., that there is an equilibrium level of wages which is determined by the cost of production of the means of subsistence. The standard of living of workers in terms of the real goods and services which their wages can buy was regarded as constant. Higher wages, more generous poor relief, or any other "artificial" interference aimed at increasing the share of the poor, can only result in a higher reproduction rate. Capital formation is reduced because profit is reduced. The reduction of profit is aggravated by the increased share which goes to landlords, for the population increase forces up rent. Wages, in terms of means of subsistence, soon return to their original level. Thus any intervention aimed at an increase in the standard of living of the workers is doomed to failure because of their natural urge to procreate. The poor would always stay poor, only the rich would be less rich.

. . . whether Ricardo was right or wrong, we are concerned here with what he actually believed. There are several indications that Ricardo regarded the lot of the workers as regrettable but inevitable. Social utility, or at any rate a substantial part of it, was believed to be represented by the values which go to the propertied classes. In the short run one might increase social utility by taking from the rich and giving to the poor. But in the long run the poor would sink back to their lower standard and the situation as a whole would be worse, for the rich would now be somewhat poorer.[7]

When later, in the middle of the century, John Stuart Mill wrote

[6] *Ibid.*, p. 117.

[7] The argument would logically have led not only to *laissez faire* in distribution but to protection in favor of the rich; but as Ricardo's heart—as well as his basic philosophical premises—was on the side of the poor, *laissez faire* emerged as a sort of compromise. See *ibid.*, pp. 119 ff.

his *Principles of Political Economy, with Some of Their Applications to Social Philosophy,* a big change had occurred which drew away the props from under this motivation for conservative *laissez faire* in the sphere of distribution: birth control had come within sight as a possible and effective means of preventing Malthus' population law from making redistributional reforms useless. And in the decades to follow, the fall in fertility rate gradually began to catch up with the fall in the mortality rates which had already gone on for a longer time.

The economic theorists who did not want to step into too radical policy interferences from the equality doctrine could no longer have recourse to Ricardo's theory of the natural wages. In this situation they had increasingly good use for Mill's distinction, which I referred to in the preceding section. It permitted them to concentrate their attention on the problems of production and trade, by making only a general reservation in regard to distribution.

When now, after the Second World War and under the influence of the Great Awakening, the perspective of economic analysis is enlarged to encompass effectively the underdeveloped countries, Malthus' population theory again comes back to relevance. Very clearly, a large part of their populations are living on a Malthusian subsistence level, where any potential improvement in levels of income is in danger of being swallowed up by population increase.

In the richer countries the temptation must, then, be strong to question the rationality of doing anything very substantial to improve living conditions for the poorer nations: on theoretical grounds *laissez faire* may seem to be the right policy. A logical basis for neutralizing the equality doctrine can be constructed similar to Ricardo's theory of the natural wages.

In the world as it is today, however, political reasons make it increasingly difficult to stick to such a negative attitude on the level of theory and general principles. But there is a sinister reality in the population worry. And anyone who wants to take the equality ideal at all seriously has to hope and pray for lower fertility rates and has to request that measures for rapid and wide spread of birth control be made part of the economic planning for economic development of underdeveloped countries.

The Reasons for Compromise

Even apart from the population issue there are obvious reasons why any move toward straight and sudden realization of the equality doctrine would appear undesirable and, indeed, disastrous in its effects. These reasons are all founded in the existing inequalities as between people in different social strata.

Economic theory had from the earliest beginnings developed in the tradition of enlightened humanitarian rationalism and it had never given any intellectual hospitality to the reactionary belief in innate differences in quality among different groups of people. The existing differences as among different nations and, within a nation, different economic classes were caused by the environment and, more specifically, by earlier economic inequalities. Nevertheless, it is clear that, whatever the cause, the differences, and in particular the differences in productive capacities, support the continued existence of the economic inequalities. Any attempt at a large and rapid change toward greater equality would break institutional continuity.

Its immediate effects would be disorganization and a decrease in production of goods and services. It is with this motivation that Alfred Marshall concluded: ". . . that therefore it is the part of responsible men to proceed cautiously and tentatively in abrogating or modifying even such rights as may seem to be inappropriate to the ideal conditions of social life." [8]

A rational equalization policy necessarily implies a time-consuming social process, particularly if the assumption is the desirability of peaceful change by means of gradual reforms. Even after the decisions in favor of reforms have been taken, large-scale inequalities will have to remain in existence for a long period if a decrease in production is to be prevented. This is the problem which for a century and more has been discussed in economic theory—

[8] *Principles of Economics,* 7th ed., Macmillan, London, 1916, p. 48.

though mostly only in a static equilibrium setting—as the conflict between more equal distribution and higher productivity.

In Marshall's formulation:[9] "Taking it for granted that a more equal distribution of wealth is to be desired, how far would this justify changes in the institutions of property, or limitations of free enterprise even when they would be likely to diminish the aggregate of wealth?"

Marshall stressed that the great economists have all the time upheld the equality ideal:

> The fact is that nearly all the founders of modern economics were men of gentle and sympathetic temper, touched with the enthusiasm of humanity. They cared little for wealth for themselves; they cared much for its wide diffusion among the masses of the people. . . . They were without exception devoted to the doctrine that the wellbeing of the whole people should be the ultimate goal of all private effort and all public policy. . . . The rights ofproperty, as such, have not been venerated by those master minds who have built up economic science.[10]

To develop his ideals, according to Marshall, "the economist needs imagination:"

> But most of all he needs caution and reserve in order that his advocacy of ideals may not outrun his grasp of the future. . . . [The founders of modern economics] appeared cold, because they would not assume the responsibility of advocating rapid advances on untried paths. . . . Their caution was perhaps a little greater than necessary: for the range of vision even of the greatest seers of that age was in some respects narrower than is that of most educated men in the present time.[11]

The fact that the great economists, as Marshall correctly emphasized, did not have a vision for social reforms which quite matched their egalitarian ideals, and that therefore their thinking was dominated not only by sound but also merely apparently sound reasons why economic inequalities had to be tolerated, at least provisionally,

[9] *Ibid.*, p. 41.
[10] *Ibid.*, pp. 47 f.
[11] *Ibid.*, pp. 46 ff.

naturally made it somewhat easier for the wealthier classes to resist the strivings for equality and, in particular, made it easier for them to do it with a better conscience.

The Dynamics of Equalization

The further fact that, as exemplified in the quotation from Marshall above, the equality issue was raised in simple static terms as a question of redistribution of income and wealth and as a choice between a more equal distribution and a lower level of productivity also contributed to decreasing the attractiveness of doing anything in the direction of equalization. It would endanger economic progress in terms of the total volume of production out of which everybody's share should come. It was thus easier to believe that the interests even of the poor would be better served by abstaining from redistributional reforms as they were holding back production.

This view is, however, entirely static. If we seek to learn from what has actually happened in the richer countries which during the past half century have proceeded far in the direction of greater equality of opportunity we reach a dynamic theory: that the realization of more equal opportunities has been needed to spur and sustain economic progress as well as to make good the assumptions of social democracy. A corollary to this is the important fact that in a progressive society—characterized by both redistributional reforms and economic growth, as the two types of social changes mutually support each other by circular causation—the improvement of the lot of the poor often can be achieved without substantial sacrifices from those who are better off and is sometimes not only compatible with, but a condition for, the attainment of higher levels in all income brackets, including the higher ones.

But this dynamic theory is now emerging more as an afterthought. It never played much of a role in economic theory or even, until quite recently, in the popular and political advocacy of redistributional reforms. The reforms were continuously motivated primarily in terms of social justice, with the implication that the better situated classes had to pay for them by accepting a lowering of their own living standards. And the question could then be asked and was, as a matter of fact, continually asked: How far could this be done without injustice, and without slackening the energies of the leaders of progress? [12] As we remember, another question asked until very recently even in our most advanced and enlightened countries was this one: Would not the motives to work and save in the lower income groups slacken when they were relieved from pressing wants and economic insecurity?

Other Competing Valuations

Moreover, even apart from the question of productivity, the equality ideal rules only on a very general plane in the valuation sphere and even there is not the only valuation. In the case of specific issues, relating more directly to the concrete choices of everyday human living, the equality ideal will often be almost lost, as there are always a great number of other valuations and as some of them conflict with it. Actual attitudes are always composite ones, and human behavior is always a moral compromise.[13]

A basic fact is, of course, that people who are better off have vested interests to protect. They are, therefore, opportunistically perceptive for every possibility of a valuation which is competing with the equality ideal and every belief which can neutralize it. This gives emotional backing to the belief in innate differences in quality between the rich and the poor. It strengthens the appeal of all such arguments which inhibit the drawing of practical inferences from the equality ideal—for instance, the static theory of the conflict between the rise in productivity and redistributional reforms.

If I insist that, nevertheless, the influence of the general equality

---

[12] *Ibid.*, p. 41.

[13] That human behavior typically is the outcome of a moral compromise of heterogeneous valuations, operating on various planes of generality and rising in various degrees and at different occasions to the level of consciousness, is a most important fact. It implies that the notion "attitude," which the social psychologists use and which was more definitely formulated by W. I. Thomas in the methodological note to his *The Polish Peasant at Home and Abroad* is a clear misconception of reality if it implies homogeneity. See my *An American Dilemma. The Negro Problem and Modern Democracy;* Appendix I, "A Methodological Note on Valuations and Beliefs," pp. 1027 ff.

ideal should not be forgotten, I do not deny that people in the main try to safeguard their interests as they perceive them—and, indeed, that they usually succeed in modulating their conception of reality enough to preserve an excellent conscience in doing so. But, this much being conceded, I must insist on the important fact that generous impulses also are real and that they do have their influence, even if the influence is limited and at times rendered almost insignificant.

The Convenience of Ignorance

It can be observed that in the compromise between thinking and living which is normal when there is such a dramatic disparity between the equality ideal and a social reality characterized by gross inequalities people who are better off have usually done their best to keep their minds off the equality issue.

In the first place, they have tried to remain ignorant of the poverty and distress of poor people. This is true even in regard to the living conditions of the lower classes in their own national communities. Ignorance is seldom random but, instead, is highly opportunistic.[14] In every country there have been whole systems of psychological and ideological barriers protecting the well-to-do classes from knowledge of social facts which would be embarrassing to them.

Everywhere, however, the attainment of political democracy has resulted in the gradual demolition of these barriers to knowledge. This was invariably an important stage in the striving for social reforms. The spread of embarrassing knowledge is one of the consequences of the greater articulateness of the poorer classes themselves and of their organization, under the shield of democracy, into pressure groups of various types for pleading their cause and fighting for it.

In the same way, solid ignorance of the poverty of the underdeveloped world was convenient and opportune to the peoples in the richer countries. It would be worth while to analyze in some detail how they succeeded in training themselves to take abstract

[14] *Ibid.*, pp. 40 ff., 1029 *et passim.*

cognizance of the occasional starvation of many millions of human beings somewhere in Asia without really making it a part of their perception of reality.

Protected by this heavy fog of opportune ignorance, the real attitudes of sympathy actually held by people—which I referred to as forming the emotional or moral basis for the equality ideal as an ideological force in society—must be thought of as rapidly lessening in intensity as the distance from the object increases. In relation to peoples outside national boundaries and, in particular, peoples of other races, religions and cultures, living far away, the intensity easily falls to practically zero.

The trend in the richer countries during recent decades toward integration and the realization of ever-greater equality of opportunity has been narrowly nationalistic. Alfred Marshall—again to quote this great eclectic master of our science whose mind was always so sensitive in conscience questions—in the introduction to *Industry and Trade,* published just after the First World War,[15] faced this situation squarely:

> . . . the notion of national trade has been bound up with the notion of solidarity between the various members of a nation. . . .
>
> We are indeed approaching rapidly to conditions which have no close precedent in the past, but are perhaps really more natural than those which they are supplanting:—conditions under which the relations between the various industrial strata of a civilised nation are being based on reason rather than tradition. . . .
>
> . . . it is becoming clear that this [Great Britain] and every other Western country can now afford to make increased sacrifices of national wealth for the purpose of raising the quality of life throughout their whole population. A time may come when such matters will be treated as of cosmopolitan rather than national obligation: but that time is not in sight. For the practical purpose of the present and the coming generation, each country must, in the main, dispose of her own resources, and bear her own burdens.

[15] Macmillan, London, 1919, pp. 4 f.

If today in the richer countries the problems of international inequalities cannot any longer be dealt with in this complacent mood, the reason is not that people have now become more compassionate for their fellow human beings all over the world than Marshall and his contemporaries. What has happened is that the misery of those far away has been brought home to the people in the richer countries and presented as a threat to their own security.

A New Phase in the Struggle for Equality

I remarked in Chapter I that the awareness of actual economic conditions in the underdeveloped world which is now thrusting itself upon the peoples in the richer countries comes as a revelation and is embarrassing. It is first and foremost the rising revolt in the underdeveloped countries themselves which is the active force in demolishing the barriers of opportunistic ignorance in our minds.

The newly won political independence of most of these countries and the ready availability to their governments of the various international organizations as sounding boards provide for this purpose of disseminating embarrassing knowledge a substitute for the world democracy that does not exist. It is my belief that the most important function of the international organizations in the present stage of world history is to provide forums where the underprivileged countries can join together in expressing their dissatisfaction.

As long as the peoples living in the underdeveloped world were subdued and quiet their grievances could be kept away from the attention of the peoples in the richer countries by opportunistic ignorance. A new phase of the age-old struggle for greater equality —a phase in which the struggle finally encompasses the entire globe—has now begun with the Great Awakening.

I have already observed that from one point of view the Great Awakening is nothing else than the victorious spread to the peoples in the underdeveloped countries of the richer nations' inherited ideal of equality of opportunity. Those nations have themselves been sowing the seed of world revolution. And so strong are the force and the unity of a culture that, even if they now should try, they would not succeed in avoiding a continuation of this dissemination. However they turn, they will be teaching and preaching equality.

Nations are not sophisticated enough to be really cynical: even when their policies are grossly opportunistic, they will rationalize them in terms of the ideal—and they will do it in good faith. Indeed, the efforts to give respectability to vested interests by dressing them up to look like the ideal—which will always imply distorting to some extent the beliefs about reality: this is the type of irrationalism that we call rationalization—are themselves a recognition of the power of the ideal as a social force.

In the setting of Western civilization the poorer countries, once they succeed in breaking through the barriers of opportunistic ignorance, will have, as already in earlier time the poorer regions and the lower social classes within the now-richer countries, a support in the egalitarian ideal which has an emotional and moral basis in people's feelings for what is right and wrong. Whether this support will be forthcoming so soon, and be so strong, that—in analogy to what has actually happened within the richer countries themselves—the world revolution can be canalized into a process of gradual and peaceful change is a momentous question to which the future will give the solemn answer.

Equalization Upward

Such a process toward a "welfare world," where on a world scale the principle of equality of opportunity as between nations, racial and religious groups, and individuals increasingly became realized, would, like the earlier parallel development toward the national "welfare state" in the richer countries, regularly turn out to be a paying proposition also to those who are initially better off. As in the nations so in the world at large, this process would be a precondition for raising levels of production generally and not only for promoting social justice.

What is needed is not primarily a redistribution of wealth and incomes. Indeed, aid can be only a very small part of a rational international equalization program as it is of a national one. None of the schemes which have been propounded for capital aid for development of underdeveloped countries has ever amounted to taking away more than a tiny fraction of the yearly increase of national income per head in the richer countries, which implies that no real sacrifices have ever been envisaged. And no one who has advocated these aid schemes has ever hesitated in the belief that the aid would be profitable as an investment for the richer countries. A wholesale income equalization by redistribution among nations is both impossible and, I am inclined to believe, an unimportant objective.

Much more important for reaching more equal opportunities in the world are reforms which concern the ways in which the richer countries with their stronger bargaining position conduct, or fail to conduct, business with the poorer countries.[16] The reforms I am thinking of concern the market for their export products, the market in which they buy their imports, and the organization of the capital market.

The international organizations have on their agenda, or have had, a great number of proposals for concerted international action in these fields which would assist the underdeveloped countries much more than even the most generous aid schemes could ever do, while not entailing any appreciable costs for the richer countries; in most cases these policies would be in their own long-term interest as well. Progress along this line has been exceedingly slow and seems now to have been stopped altogether, as I pointed out in Chapter V. In Chapter VI I hinted at some of the explanations of the cumulative political process which has been causing the richer countries to take an increasingly negative attitude toward actions in these fields.

But I would not feel discouraged. In any case we have not the right to retreat into fatalism. Attitudes may change. And, as attitudes are based on people's beliefs, even the increase of true knowledge is not without importance. It is not excluded that awareness of the dangers inherent in their *non possumus* attitude could come to spread among the intellectual leaders in the richer countries and among the common people there.

[16] Cf. "Aid and Trade," *The American Scholar,* Spring, 1957.

Fact-Finding in the Social Sciences

I have stressed the importance for this political process toward social democracy in the world at large of the dissemination of embarrassing knowledge. It is natural to ask what role the social scientists are playing in these efforts.

It might be expected that the social scientists would have been a mighty force for rectifying false and opportunistic popular beliefs. The inherited equality doctrine, placed at the roots of all modern economic and social theories, should have led the social scientists in succeeding generations to make it a main task of theirs to seek to lay bare the existing economic inequalities and to explain why they had come into existence. This expectation would be the more natural as we know that many, perhaps most, social scientists even up to our own time were originally led to their studies because of their interest in social reform.[17]

The social scientists could also be expected to have been less able to remain in opportunistic ignorance, at least in the fields in which they were specializing. Admitting that they too have their blinkers—corresponding to their share of the prejudices of a community at a particular time, what Marshall called their narrower range of vision—it is difficult to see how they could help venturing into disinterested research now and then.

And even if they started out with opportunistically biased views, their analysis was under some discipline both from the facts and from logic. Thus, the experimental psychologists, who half a century ago first set out to measure intelligence, actually shared with their contemporaries the reactionary belief in innate differences of quality between different groups of people. They assumed therefore great average differences in intelligence between rich and poor, whites

[17] See my earlier quotations from Marshall, which I believe are true in characterizing the moral inclinations of economists in the line of the great tradition. In the Marshall Library in Cambridge, England, there is a little painting which had belonged to Alfred Marshall, portraying a poorly clad, soulful and sympathetic young man. It is said that Marshall kept this picture near his desk in order that he should constantly be reminded that all work in economics should have as its ultimate purpose the improvement of the conditions of the poorer classes.

and Negroes, men and women. It is one of the great triumphs of scientific endeavor that the more they labored to measure these differences, and the more they perfected their methods in doing so, the less differences they were able to ascertain.

There is a deep wisdom in the Bible's saying: "He that seeketh findeth." But under the discipline of the scientific truth-ethos, the psychologists did not find what they had set out to seek. They were not able to draw the inferences they wished to draw. They came to conclusions contrary to their hypotheses and they had to change them. Scientific research led to the refutation of the assumption of innate differences of quality between different groups of human beings—this reactionary belief which, as I pointed out, had been counterbalancing the equality ideal.

Undoubtedly, over the decades the steady growth of ascertained, analyzed and organized data has had a mighty influence in the process of breaking down the opportunistic barriers which were protecting people from embarrassing knowledge and has thus been a force for a growing rationality in their world outlook. Time and time again in all countries individual social scientists have also ventured to stir up people's conscience on a specific issue, with the result that sometimes a permanent mutation in what was up till then common and comfortable ignorance could be registered.

Usually, however, the social scientists, even as fact-gatherers, can be seen to work in the wake of political events rather than in advance of them. The present intensive efforts in studying the problems of the underdeveloped countries did not precede public concern over these problems and still less did our research cause this concern. On the contrary, this new direction of our research was itself caused and inspired by the pressure of the events which gave political weight to those issues.

When, however, in one way or another an inequality issue is once opened for public debate, usually social science research will diligently push ahead and do a sort of finishing job: it will continue to break down and sweep away the remnants of the opportunistic barriers protecting people from embarrassing knowledge. That is what to an increasing extent is now actually happening in regard to the growing awareness of the poverty and distress in under-developed countries. And the inherited equality doctrine will continuously give force and energy to this process.

The Traditionalism of Theory

If in the social sciences fact-gathering research, while it seldom opens up entirely new vistas, thus tends to reinforce every movement—once it has had an independent start—toward greater recognition of such social facts as are embarrassing because of their conflict with established ideals, I am afraid that the same cannot be said about those vast structures of concepts and generalizations which we call theories.

They show generally a much stronger conservative and traditionalistic bias. Not only do they usually fail by themselves to develop in a direction which opens up new vistas: they tend, on the contrary, to inhibit us from looking through those vistas which are opened up and widened by other social forces, including fact-finding. This traditionalism of theory is also, indeed, a main explanation why fact-finding research does not demonstrate more daring and originality—why it so regularly moves in the wake of the political events and so seldom anticipates them.

In general, I am impressed by the power of tradition in most theoretical speculations, and particularly so in the economic field. Even when we are not aware of our bondage we are all more or less under the influence of certain very general ideas or patterns of thought which we have inherited from long ago. At one time or another they were all solidified into definite doctrines; but even now when some of these doctrines are not accepted any longer, and often even when they have actually been refuted, they still prevail in the form of vaguer predilections and exert considerable influence on our way of thinking. Even the scholar who breaks new ground in economic theory is usually original only on one particular front line of thinking, where by exerting exceptional genius and will power he succeeds in beating down the traditional predilections, while in other respects he is a traditionalist.[18]

[18] I might be permitted in this connection to make a contribution to the growing treasure of Keynesiana.

Our tools of analysis have been molded within the tradition of these doctrines and predilections. We have had them pressed upon our work in the form of a certain approach to problems, a particular manner of looking at things. This determines broadly what questions we ask and how we ask them. It therefore inhibits our imagination and, as I have just said, this frustration of originality in turn affects our fact-finding research.

These inherited and dominating predilections of economic theory are, however, vague and abstract enough to provide ample leeway for a great display of scientific acumen and learnedness and for a measure of inventiveness and controversy. We have in this tradition become particularly delighted in such mental exercises as are "purely scientific," in the sense that they have no great and immediate practical import.

These predilections are all to a degree value-loaded: many of them, as we shall find, serve pressing needs for rationalization. This increases their influence over our intellectual exertions and tends—unless we work with explicit value premises—to protect them from our close awareness and critical attention.

The "Realism of Conservatism"

In the next chapter I will attempt to give a condensed analysis of these predilections which in a usually uncontrolled manner de-

---

Sometime soon after the publication of his *General Theory*, Keynes visited us in Stockholm and spoke at a gathering of the Club of Economists which had been founded around Knut Wicksell when, toward the end of the First World War, he moved to Stockholm from Lund as professor emeritus; at the time of Keynes's visit Wicksell had already been dead for some ten years.

Not surprisingly, Keynes had chosen as topic for his talk: "Heresies in Economics." After his talk one after another of the youngest members of our Club took the floor and accused Keynes of being too classical on this and that point. To this day I do not know if there had been a planned collusion to tease Keynes when standing in his favorite pose as the heretic, or if it just happened.

Keynes met his young critics with open delight—implying that the criticism directed against him for being too classical, though exaggerated, was a particularly bright and amusing idea—only gradually very slightly darkened by some easily understandable irritation on the part of Keynes, who had been brought out of his role.

termine the mental climate in which we work. My main interest will be focused on their logical interrelations and their relations to the historically given philosophical fundament of economic theory.

The general point I want to make here, before closing this chapter, is this: to the extent that our reasoning about economic matters comes under the influence of these old and powerful predilections this will regularly have the effect of turning our attention away from the equality issue. It will tend to move our practical and political conclusions in the direction of the idea that everything will come out to the satisfaction of all if the natural forces of the market are left their free play—which, of course, also implies that it is more permissible to forget about the equality postulate.

Politically these doctrines and predilections thus represent a conservative bias and particularly so in regard to questions of the distribution of incomes and wealth. There were many radical writers who insisted on studying social reality from the point of view of the equality ideal. But the main line of development of economic theory was laid out by writers who were inclined to turn their interest away from this issue.

And there is an explanation for this. As long as economic thinking had a metaphysical foundation and a teleological intent—as it very definitely had among the classical economists and to a large extent still has among contemporary economists—there ruled an arbitrary but effective principle of historical selection, which I have referred to as founded upon "the realism of conservatism." [19] The conservatively inclined writers, steered in their analysis by a conception of an ideal society more like the one we see, could actually often deliver a superior explanation of social reality in causal terms. This theoretical superiority of conservative thinking is, of course, entirely fortuitous. It does not imply that conservative political valuations are in any sense "true" or even "truer" than the more radical ones. [20]

[19] *Ibid.*, p. 31.

[20] The way to free our thinking from this and other irrational influences from the political sphere is to work with explicit value premises. Conservative conclusions, or other conclusions, will then be seen to emerge not out of

Also, as I will exemplify in the next chapter, the basic illogicality of normative and teleological reasoning—endeavoring to objectify valuations, which cannot be done—represents a force persistently driving the philosopher and the theorist to seek refuge in the apparent simplicity of one version or another of *laissez faire*. These doctrines, if they are accepted, dispose of a host of awkward queries which would raise their heads as soon as they are given up.

These are explanations of the conservative twist of economic theory given in terms of logic. To look on the question from a different point of view, that of the sociology of knowledge, it strikes the eye immediately that all our economic speculation was for a long time almost exclusively cultivated in the social setting of the then most prosperous country, Great Britain. Thereafter, and until very recently, it was developed further by theorists who, almost without exception, were the nationals of those few countries which were rapidly progressing economically under conditions of expanding mutual trade and large movements of capital and labor. And in these countries all higher culture, including the rise of economic science, was concentrated at the centers of economic expansion.

These facts have very clearly been of importance in the selection of viewpoints and thereby also in setting the approaches for economic theory. What I am suggesting is that economic theory, as it developed, was to some extent a rationalization of the interests and the aspirations of the milieu where it grew.

The escapist tendencies of economic theory as far as the equality postulate is concerned become in this light comprehensible. Still less should it be surprising that, in particular, the problems peculiar to the underdeveloped countries tended to fade out in a pale distant haze—until in recent years they were forcefully pressed upon the world by the political and spiritual revolt of the peoples living there. All this is, indeed, very understandable, once one places oneself outside this main trend of economic speculation and looks on its development as a part of social history which needs to be explained in terms of causes and effects, like everything else that has happened.

---

pure theory but from the fact that reality is studied from certain points of view, which are defined independently of the theory.

The real mystery, which I am not in the position to solve in this context but have to take as independently given, is the opposite fact of the always clear presence and relative power of the equality doctrine. Where did this lofty ideal come from? And how could it continuously preserve its position at the basis of economic theory and our entire culture?

From one point of view the persistent tendency of economic theory to take very special precautions in order not to draw practical policy inferences from the equality doctrine, and the whole involved system of theoretical constructs built up to insulate the equality doctrine in an abstract compartment, is a sort of backhanded recognition of the sovereignty of this ideal of the right of all human beings to equality of opportunity. In a sense, economic theory had its entire structure determined by the need to protect it from this revolutionary ideal which was at its very basis.

X.

The Conservative Predilections of Economic Theory and Their Foundation in the Basic Philosophies

Antidotes to the Equality Doctrine

THE philosophies of natural law and utilitarianism, which had instilled in economic theory the ultraradical equality doctrine, at the same time furnished it with the perfect antidotes: a whole set of doctrines designed to render the equality doctrine harmless. These doctrines are all variations on a single theme, that on the whole— and with a number of reservations—everything will come out to the satisfaction of all if the natural forces of the market are left their free play—which, of course, also implies that it is more permissible to forget about the equality postulate.

Such useful logical miracles can be expected from our philosophies and theories as long as they are metaphysical. Almost by necessity, and not by choice alone, people live in moral compromise, and this implies also a considerable logical confusion; in such a situation, what they demand from their philosophies and theories as from their religions is precisely antidotes to their ideals. On the other hand, the capacity of metaphysical notions to assist in creating a semblance of harmony in thoughts and feelings, where there is in fact disharmony, and to give psychological rationalization to opportunistic interests is, at the same time, the explanation of the fact that it has proved so difficult to drive out the metaphysics from our thinking. Metaphysics serves a purpose: it meets our need for rationalization.

In the course of time the doctrines tended to evaporate into what I have called predilections. The ability of these vague inclinations to survive, and to continue to exert their influence, was based on people's opportunistic interest in escaping from the equality doctrine. Their resistance to logical criticism is undoubtedly also due to the fact that as doctrines they had once been firmly rooted in the philosophies which still provide the general form for our inherited economic theory.

Harmony of Interests

The notion of harmony of interests is a basic predilection in economic theory. It is certainly a comforting thought for those who have drawn a lucky number in life's lottery.

The idea was a clearly perceived conviction in the philosophy of natural law which served as the basis for the first construction of a general economic theory some two hundred years ago.

In utilitarianism, which soon took over the function of forming the philosophical basis for economic theory, this assumption of an existing harmony of interests became a more involved matter and was often hidden away in tacit assumptions and sometimes explicitly renounced on the level of general principles, as, for instance, by Bentham. And many of the theoretical approaches of the classical economists in England were based on a recognition of conflicting interests as, for example, Ricardo's theory of distribution.

But in the end, even in the economic thinking that was based on utilitarianism, the notion of a harmony of interests pressed itself into the practical and political conclusions as a major predilection. For it was inherent and logically necessary in the very attempt of the utilitarians to explain both actual behavior and a moral behavior in terms of the hedonistic mechanism of the sensations of pleasure and pain.

At bottom this was also an identification between "what is" and "what ought to be" and, as in the philosophy of natural law, such an identification assumes a harmony of interests in society: the differences in real life between an actually perceived utility and the morally correct one had to be explained as a "miscalculation of chances"—this expression is Bentham's. Without the assumption of a harmony of interests, the empirical philosophy of utilitarianism would lose its claim to objectivity.[1]

The further fact that the utilitarians could not in practice carry out the social calculus of pleasure and pain—which was their proclaimed method of empirically determining those policies which gave as a result the maximum "general welfare"—by necessity brought this assumption of harmony up from the level of epistemology to the level of practical discussion in connection with various topical political issues.[2] If identity of individual interests could be assumed, there would be no need for ascertaining them more precisely and for adding them up to a social sum in order to establish the conditions for its maximization, as these conditions are assumed as given. However, on this level the assumption was, then as now, often hidden as an implicit link in the chain of argument.

In both these closely related philosophies, from which all our modern economic and social theory has branched out, it was stressed that social institutions, as they functioned when under the influence of state "interferences," prevented the natural harmony of interests from being realized. The entire discussion between the more radical and the more conservative writers for two centuries, when it is brought to the pivotal point, turns around the question of what, and how much, prior institutional change would be necessary to bring society to the natural state of harmony of interests.[3] Even Marx is no exception to this generalization, though his major interest became focused on the dynamic process as society moved from one stage to another and not on the end result.

It was, however, mainly the conservatives who came to determine the development of economic theory. As I mentioned at the end of the preceding chapter, the fate of their theories profited from the

[1] *The Political Element in the Development of Economic Theory*, pp. 44, 48 *et passim*.

[2] *Ibid.*, pp. 43 *et passim*.

[3] *Ibid.*, pp. 71 ff., 106 ff. *et passim*.

accident that they happened to be conservative; for this implied that they were interested in a natural state of harmony which, to them, was fairly like the world they saw. Their teleological analysis of social reality became, therefore, more easily acceptable because it mirrored the *status quo*. This is what I referred to as the "realism of conservatism."

Today we might feel ourselves far away from the confident faith of the old philosophers in an intrinsic harmony of interests in the world as we see it, or as it would be after certain purifying reforms. But if we scrutinize carefully the way we are apt to formulate and motivate our most general policy opinions in regard to their expected effects, or if we similarly analyze leading articles in the press, party programs and the speeches during an election campaign, or a debate in the General Assembly of the United Nations, and likewise if we search our own economic theories and ask for an explanation as to why they approach problems in the way they do, and if we then succeed in keeping the distance necessary to discern the broad pattern of our reasoning, we shall be surprised to find what a powerful hold over our thinking this old doctrine of the harmony of interests has maintained.

Laissez Faire

Another but slightly different predilection, closely related to the interest harmony doctrine, is the antistate and, indeed, the "anti-organization" bias or, as it is usually known, the laissez-faire inclination.

In the philosophy both of natural law and of utilitarianism, atomistic individualism was a conscious assumption, stressed in protest against earlier and contemporary philosophies which tended to give to the state and other collective bodies an organic nature and, indeed, a kind of personality with independent, if limited, interests, rights and duties. The hedonistic psychology was thus already implied in the philosophy of natural right; in the empiricist utilitarian philosophy it was elaborated and laid down as the basis for the whole endeavor of calculating the "general welfare" as a sum of individual interests. The specific political bias to which I refer springs from the fact that this calculation was made upon the further assumption—or adjusted to fit the further assumption—of interest harmony in society.[4]

To the physiocrats as the early exponents of the philosophy of natural law the laissez-faire bias was programmatic: to them the explanation why the "natural order" of the harmony of individual interests did not materialize in full perfection was mainly the "interferences" of the state and other collective bodies. As I pointed out in Chapter IV, in their time the state and its institutional substructure of organized interests was also not of the type our modern "welfare state" is approaching but might very generally be characterized, instead, as an "oppressor state."

Bentham, unlike the physiocrats, started out with strong condemnation of the aprioristic metaphysics implied in the assumption of natural laws and conceived of his own philosophical exertions as the working out, on the basis of empirically ascertained sensations, of general rules for public morale and legislation, i.e., interferences by the state. But in the economic field, by intrinsic logic, the result of this—as of any other attempt at founding moral and political views solely upon an observation of facts—was, for reasons already suggested, a relapse into the doctrine of a natural harmony of individual interests which, in its turn, carries an inextricable antistate and antiorganization bias. This is more clearly the situation if the analysis is focused on an ideal society not very different from the actual one, which on the whole was Bentham's approach and very definitely the approach of those authors, all of them Bentham's followers, who, thanks to the "realism of conservatism," came to determine the main trend in the development of economic theory.

To Marx, however, the society he saw was very far from ideal. He analyzed the inner contradictions of the early capitalistic society around him. As a German scholar and, in particular, a student of Hegel, the notion of a stable equilibrium never came to fetter his

[4] The prolific modern "welfare economics" moves inescapably under the same spell, attempting by individualistic psychology to reach a metaphysical goal, determined in advance by the predilections and, more particularly, the harmony doctrine, which is logically inherent, as otherwise the objectivity of the welfare notion would be lost (see above).

mind; this undoubtedly helped him to demonstrate much originality
in his studies of the cyclical and structural changes. The doctrine of
harmony of interests he criticized vehemently. Indeed, he attempted
to view the whole of history as a sequence of class struggles, each
one differently staged because of the changing modes of production;
he dealt with the state as the instrument of oppression by the ruling
classes. But with all that, Marx ended up with the sweet anarchistic
vision of the "state of liberty" attained when, after the final revolution of the proletariat, the state would have "withered away." Apart
from the controversial questions of the correct exegesis of these statements, the significant thing is that Marx never worked out a system
of organized economic policies to be carried out after the revolution: the notion of "economic planning," now recognized as the
true shibboleth of socialism, did not play any important role in his
thinking.

No one in the entire tradition of economic speculation as this
speculation developed after the Enlightenment, not even the critics
of our social order and our social theories, seems to have escaped
altogether this common predilection for individualistic atomism in
theory and antistate and antiorganization bias in practical conclusions. Our modern thinking has on the whole been developed by
theorists who, with all their facilities, usually did not have the
revolutionary intellectual will and powers of a Bentham or a Marx
to view from a distance the old theories they had inherited and to
dare original construction of their own. We should therefore not be
surprised to find that recent economic thinking also has tended to
remain within the bounds of these vague predilections.

As our research resources have increased we have been able to
expand tremendously our empirical knowledge of social and political
institutions. But our general economic theories, even, and not least,
in their econometric diffusion into the less accessible corners from
Walras, Jevons and Edgeworth onward, have largely remained faithful to the old predilections. This is of particular importance, since
general theories have always had a closer relation to policy prescriptions than empirical studies. The empirical studies of the
institutions have meanwhile, in this climate of basic intellectual

predilections, mostly either shown a tendency to adjust themselves to theory or remained strangely pointless.

The Free Trade Doctrine

The free trade doctrine, which I mention here as the third of the main predilections of economic theory, is usually presented as a conclusion from theoretical analysis; in reality it is, however, the matrix into which the entire analysis has been molded. It is a more specific corollary of the assumption of harmony of interests and expresses that assumption's inherent antistate and antiorganization bias. All these general ideas are interlocking; they are indeed only differently adapted modalities of the same dominant structuralization of thought which I am here trying to characterize.

The practical triumph of the free trade doctrine is the fact that even the severest critics of the general policy line of noninterference usually find it difficult to free themselves from its fascination.[5] Thus the motivation for an interference in production or trade is ordinarily presented not simply as a means to an end but in the form of reasons why, under special circumstances, an exception from the free trade doctrine should be accepted.

The free trade doctrine, in fact, has been allowed to set the terms of reference not only for the theory of international trade and commercial policy but, more generally, for all discussion of state or group interferences in economic life. The burden of proof is always supposed to lie with the interventionist.

In point of logic this is, indeed, somewhat astonishing. As a theory, the free trade doctrine is not tenable.[6] Apart from this—and accepting for the sake of argument that the doctrine is valid in some sense—the practical free trade postulate, as presented by the theorists when emerging from their analysis, is always equipped with a large number of abstract assumptions and reservations.[7] The question then arises what a general *practical* postulate for *concrete*

[5] *Ibid.*, pp. 104 ff.
[6] *Ibid.*, pp. 129 ff.
[7] *Ibid.*, pp. 134 ff.

action really means when it is delimited by *abstract* assumptions and reservations.

One of the assumptions is particularly awkward: free competition. Such a situation has never existed and the actual trends are away from it. Generally it is not even possible to decide whether a particular policy measure in a particular country would bring us nearer to, or take us further away from, the purely fictitious state of free competition.

Why, then, in pure logic, should a policy of inaction be given the benefit of doubt? Why should the free trade doctrine be the one idea to be allowed to set the stage? Why should interferences be judged by the criterion whether they are justified as exceptions? Why should not the rule be simply that, as always, we should be careful to have our facts straight and our reasoning correct in terms of means and ends? These were questions I raised thirty years ago, and further study and experience have only confirmed me in my critical thoughts.

The Equilibrium Concept

A closing link in the system of inherited doctrines and predilections in economic theory is the concept of stable equilibrium. In Chapter I, I counted to the credit of the equilibrium notion that it represents a convenient means to comprehend and demonstrate in a simple fashion the universal interdependence among all the factors in the economic system, and also that it constitutes an almost indispensable logical step in many economic arguments.

Together with some other assumptions, the assumption of stable equilibrium has, however, also a function to fill as a necessary device when giving expression and logical "proof" to the doctrines and predilections analyzed in this chapter, for instance to the free trade doctrine. The equilibrium concept has therefore in the metaphysical framework of our inherited economic theory retained a teleological significance above the simple and technical purpose of being a chosen theoretical tool useful for the analysis of social reality.

The notion of stable equilibrium also has run through our whole economic and social speculation during the past two hundred years and has until this day determined the main concepts of all the social sciences, and not only economics. From what I have said it becomes understandable why there has always been an urge to give a positive value connotation to the state of equilibrium—as two hundred years ago to the natural order, which from this point of view is only a special case—and to give a negative one to disequilibrium or "disorganization," "maladjustment," "social lag" and "crisis," to mention here only a few of the near-synonyms adopted in various directions in the different social science disciplines.

Reality was assumed normally not to be in equilibrium. The doctrine is, however, that equilibrium nevertheless had a "virtual reality" as the state toward which actual reality, despite all disturbances, ever tended to move. This virtual equilibrium state could at the same time be utilized as a norm in forming value judgments concerning actual reality. This was the way of thinking of the physiocrats and the classical authors and the idea reached its most comprehensively elaborated refinement in the neoclassical general equilibrium theory.

Knut Wicksell used to point out, however, that there are many alternatively possible equilibrium concepts which could be useful in theoretical analysis. That one used in economic equilibrium analysis of the classical type is only one of these: the stable equilibrium which may be illustrated by the hanging pendulum or a ball at the bottom of a bowl and which, if attained and not further disturbed, would imply that things remained motionless.

One of the other equilibrium notions can be illustrated by a cylinder rolling on a plane surface: it may come to rest anywhere; if friction were entirely absent it would continue to roll in the same direction with unchanged speed, and that movement would then be its equilibrium.

A third equilibrium notion is the "liable state" of balancing forces in which a pencil would remain, if one succeeded in placing it upright, on its end; pushing it over would, however, cause an accelerated movement away from the original state of balancing forces.

Many of the theoretical advances in economics in the past two generations have, as a matter of fact, been made by departing from the inherited stable equilibrium notion. Large portions of Keynesian and post-Keynesian analysis—though not the general theoretical framework—have this character. Wicksell's analysis of the cumulative and accelerating process away from monetary equilibrium when the "natural" rate of interest came to differ from the market rate is another example, and an earlier one.

Even before this, Marshall's theory of external economies and, indeed, much earlier analysis of increasing returns had reached outside the field dominated by the notion of stable equilibrium. The earliest classical authors themselves had, besides their short-term equilibrium theory, an analysis of long-term economic development —in fact they had more of it than the neoclassical authors—and part of it went far outside the framework of equilibrium analysis. The present lively discussion on the economic development of underdeveloped countries, including the building of dynamic models, also often moves outside the theoretical framework of the stable equilibrium approach.

In recent decades much effort has gone into systematic attempts to build up a dynamic economic theory. In these new approaches the stable equilibrium notion has by logical analysis been relativized and cut down to its proper significance as a very abstract, almost crude, and usually unrealistic theoretical assumption.

But the notion of a stable equilibrium is in our tradition much more than a theoretical assumption; it is a hardened and sturdy predilection, and this is the explanation why, in spite of all the critical onslaughts, it has retained much of its hold over our theoretical approaches, often more than we find it convenient to be fully conscious of. In particular, the huge and dominating structure of the theory of international trade has in the most part stubbornly remained an equilibrium theory. This is, as I shall discuss further in the next chapter, a principal reason why it cannot provide the basis for a valid theory of underdevelopment and development and of international inequalities.

The stable equilibrium notion, even when it is no longer held consistently as a doctrine, has remained a scientific bias steering our theoretical approaches. It contains, and is animated by, all the other main predilections of economic theory mentioned above: the idea of interest harmony, the antistate and antiorganization inclination, and the free trade presumption.

A Blind Spot

I have characterized these predilections of economic theory as antidotes to the equality doctrine placed at the basis of this theory. No logical conciliation is possible: the conflict becomes hidden by the suppression of the equality doctrine. As an exemplification of this general rule, and as an introduction to the next chapter dealing with the theory of international trade, some short comments may be appropriately inserted concerning the blind spot developed by the classical economists in England in regard to the interests of foreign nations.

An essential element of the equality doctrine was, of course, the assertion common to both the philosophers of natural law and the utilitarians that, in calculating the general welfare, everyone should be counted as one and nobody as more or less than one. To this principle corresponds the aspiration of those philosophies, and also of economic theory as it developed at the end of the eighteenth and the beginning of the nineteenth century, to be general philosophies and theories. Indeed, the determination to tolerate no national limitations to their thinking was one of the intellectual ambitions of the writers of this epoch which represented its glory and which entitles it to be remembered as the age of Enlightenment. It distinguished all their speculation from most of what had gone before.

One of the implications of this way of thinking is, naturally, that the concern of economic theory must be the interests—at bottom the "pleasures" and "plains"—of human beings in general all over the globe. It would not be logically compatible with the philosophical foundations of economic theory that its concern should be confined to the interests of the members of any particular national branch of mankind. In principle this is evident and was seen to be evident; it was never explicitly denied by writers in the great classical tradition. For two hundred years it has given a cosmopolitan flavor to our most abstract concepts and pronouncements in economics.

In a queer way, however, the equality doctrine, in so far as it concerned international relations, was from the beginning almost entirely blotted out from practical attention and much more completely so than it ever was in regard to purely national issues. A sort of opportunistic blind spot developed to serve this purpose. As Professor Lionel Robbins has rightly pointed out,[8] it would be difficult to find a single case where the English classical economists actually recommended that Britain should make a sacrifice for the welfare of the rest of the world. When, for instance, they recommended free trade as a general policy, it was not on the ground that free trade would be for the good of the world but because it would be in the interest of their own country.

The important point I want to stress is that the English classical economists, when tackling international economic problems, did not set as their highest moral and political notion, directing their analysis, the welfare of mankind but rather the welfare of the British nation. From their basic philosophies and their abstract value theories, the former procedure would, however, have been the logically correct one. In choosing the narrower welfare criterion they acted against their own very explicit basic principles, and it thus becomes understandable why their writings are so evasive on this point.

On a very general plane we have here also an illustration of the functioning of the free trade doctrine as a means of psychological rationalization. For, if it can be assumed that free trade would also be in the interest of all other countries as well as of Britain—as a general proposition and with many exceptions of which the literature takes due account without letting them influence the general doctrine—the choosing of the narrower welfare criterion would not be damaging to anybody. And, indeed, it does not then become so necessary to be too explicit about whose welfare was assumed to be desirable in the analysis. The free trade doctrine thus made it more

[8] *The Theory of Economic Policy,* Macmillan, London, 1952, pp. 9 ff.

possible for the classical economists to avoid exposing themselves
and their readers to the existence of the blind spot in their thinking.

On a deeper emotional level, i.e., in the setting of the public
conscience in the advanced countries where the theory was being
developed, this blind spot is, of course, related to the traditional
callousness toward foreigners which I commented upon in the preceding chapter and which the abstract speculations during the Enlightenment period and later did not change very much.

XI.

A Note on the Theory of International Trade and the Inequality Problem

Factor Price Equalization

A STUDY, however intensive, of the theory of international trade would not provide much of an explanation in causal terms of how the facts of international economic inequalities have come into existence and why there is a tendency for the inequalities to grow. On the contrary, this theory would have led one to expect that international inequalities should not be as large as they are and that they should be shrinking rather than growing.

"The fact that many underdeveloped countries do not derive the advantages from modern transportation and commerce that theory seems to demand is one of the most pertinent facts in the present international situation and cannot be easily dismissed"—I am quoting from a recent paper by a Swedish economist, the late Folke Hilgerdt,[1] whose outstanding contributions to our ideas about the "network of international trade" and related matters, made when he was a member of the Economic Secretariat of the League of Nations, are now classic texts.

Hilgerdt refers to the fact that huge movements of labor and capital from Europe have transformed the plains in the temperate belts into "white man's land" with rapid and sustained economic

[1] "Uses and Limitations of International Trade in Overcoming Inequalities in World Distribution of Population and Resources," *World Population Conference,* Rome, 1954 (to be published).

development and high and rising levels of living. "Yet the gradual filling of the 'empty spaces' has not reduced the pressure of population in, for instance, Asia's over-populated regions where labour is most abundant." For more than a quarter of a century large-scale movements of factors of production have now almost stopped. But Hilgerdt's point is that, even in the era when such movements did take place, they did not function as a force for equalization.

Let us remember, however, that according to the classical doctrine movements of labor and capital between countries would not be necessary to bring about a development toward an equalization of factor prices and, consequently, incomes. In fact, the theory of international trade was largely developed on the abstract assumption of international immobility of all factors of production. That trade itself initiated a tendency toward a gradual and partial equalization of factor prices in different countries, and not only the price relations, was already implicit in the exposition of the classical economists, though their method of stating the law of comparative costs in terms of a single factor, labor—which, however, could have different "qualities"—turned the emphasis in other directions.

In Eli F. Heckscher's paper on the equalizing influences of trade on factor prices and Bertil Ohlin's restatement of the classical theory of international trade in terms of a general equilibrium theory of the Lausanne school type and his further development of Heckscher's thoughts on the equalization of factor prices,[2] trade appears even more clearly as a substitute for, or an alternative to, factor movements. The more explicit stress on the equilibrating and equalizing effects of international trade represents a main interest in the new approach. Trade would permit industrial activity to adapt itself to the localization of natural and population resources in different regions and different countries. The result should be that

[2] Eli F. Heckscher, "The Effect of Foreign Trade on the Distribution of Income," *Readings in the Theory of International Trade*, selected by a committee of the American Economic Association, Allen & Unwin, London, 1950 (translation from the Swedish original of 1919); Bertil Ohlin, *Interregional and International Trade*, Harvard University Press, Cambridge, 1933.

the relative scarcity of labor and capital would become less different.

Upon this foundation there has in the postwar years been a lively discussion between the econometricians elaborating—under specific, abstract and static, conditions—the relative effectiveness of this tendency to equalization of factor prices in different countries as a result of international trade.[3]

We thus see the strange thing that in recent decades, while international economic inequalities have been growing and recently also have become a more and more pressing practical concern in international politics, the theory of international trade has developed in the direction of stressing ever more the idea that trade initiated a tendency toward a gradual equalization of factor prices and incomes as between different countries.

The inadequacy of a theory given such a direction of interest to explain reality cannot be accounted for by pointing to the relative breakdown of the multilateral trading system which functioned before the First World War, a change which is related as both effect and cause to the increase of restrictions on international trade and payments. For, as Hilgerdt observed, a confrontation of the theory of international trade with the facts of international inequalities in the period before 1914 reveals the same discord.

The Inadequacy of the Theory to Explain the Facts

It is an understatement to say that the theory of international trade does not furnish us with a model or logical mechanism representing a system of rational hypotheses which can be used for explaining why and how the huge economic inequalities between different countries have come to exist and why they tend to grow. This theory has, instead, been given a twist, and—*mirabile dictu*—in very recent years increasingly so, in the direction of suggesting a situation and a development trend quite contrary to the actual ones.

[3] The recent discussion of the problem of factor price equalization as a result of international trade was initiated by Professor Paul A. Samuelson in two articles in the *Economic Journal*, 1948 and 1949; for fuller reference see Svend Laursen, "Production Functions and the Theory of International Trade," *The American Economic Review*, 1955, pp. 540 ff.

Under these circumstances it should not surprise us that, on the whole, the literature is curiously devoid of attempts to relate the facts of international inequalities and the problems of under-development and development to the theory of international trade. Hilgerdt could have raised a claim to originality merely on the ground of having posed this question in the paper I have cited.

Professor Jacob Viner, the foremost exponent in our generation of the great theoretical tradition of the classical economists, gave his lectures in Brazil the provocative title: *International Trade and Economic Development* [4]—but he did not raise *this* issue. Viner, in fact, singles out the problem of economic development of under-developed countries for separate discussion in a last chapter where he makes many interesting, though rather disconnected, observations and suggestions about poverty. In that chapter he also touches upon various international relations: gives reasons why foreign capital will probably not be available on any large scale, reassures the underdeveloped countries, perhaps a little too readily, against any general adverse bias in the movement of their terms of trade, and points to the possibility open to them, *nota bene* with good fiscal and monetary management, of counteracting the effects of the wide fluctuations in their export prices.

But the theory of international trade appears only very occasion-ally and then in certain general pronouncements which seem some-what lost and out of place.[5] In the five earlier chapters he renders a

[4] The Clarendon Press, Oxford, 1953.

[5] For example: "In a predominantly agricultural country rapid growth of population unaccompanied by proportionate growth in demand for its agri-cultural products will under free-market conditions bring spontaneously into action forces tending to industrialize the country by making agricultural production less remunerative" (*ibid.*, p. 113). This is a very inaccurate description of what has actually taken place, and is taking place, in the underdeveloped parts of the world.

One particular point where thinking in terms of the equilibrium assump-tion leads entirely astray is the idea that "free market conditions bring spontaneously into action forces" tending to equilibrate industry and agri-culture. As a matter of fact, even if population growth and pressure on the land should come to reduce marginal productivity of labor in agriculture to zero, labor would not be available for industrialization except for a wage delightfully readable account of his, on the whole, orthodox ideas about a host of problems in the international trade field but has astonishingly little to say about what the reader would expect from the title of the book: the relation between trade and development—except again in the form of intelligent innuendoes scattered throughout the text.[6]

Unrealistic Assumptions

It is an interesting question to ask for an explanation of this strange isolation of the theory of international trade from the facts of economic life.

A main explanation is undoubtedly that this theory to a higher degree than any other part of economic speculation has remained faithful to the heritage of the classical economists. I have already referred to their blind eye for the international equality problem. The inherited doctrines and predilections—the free trade doctrine, the laissez-faire bias, and the notion of harmony of interests—and the system of static assumptions basic to those theoretical constructs have been given freer play in the theory of international trade than anywhere else.

The theory of international trade and, indeed, economic theory in general were thus never developed to comprehend the reality of

---

which is—comparatively—high. Costs and prices in industry do not reflect real opportunity (or displacement) costs.

[6] Viner may answer by stressing that he assumes "free market conditions"; but with a very inclusive logical content the point is that such an assumption is totally unrealistic. Indeed, it remains an unanswered question what precisely this assumption means in the actual cultural, social, psychological and economic conditions in underdeveloped countries; if this question is not answered—and I believe it cannot be answered—this whole way of thinking remains meaningless; and it becomes wrong if any inferences as to reality are drawn. Viner probably agrees with this, for, as I point out in the text, he does not in fact attempt any consistent use of any theory in his treatment of the development problems of underdeveloped countries. Furthermore, even if there are profits to be made in industry there are no entrepreneurs to seize the opportunity; or those there are have not the skill to do it so that the profit would be realized. Even more fundamentally, the search for profit is not as universal a motive for human behavior as the classics supposed; in particular, the appreciation is slight for that type of profit which accrues from production and long-term investment.

great and growing economic inequalities and of the dynamic processes of underdevelopment and development. Economic theory was, indeed, never focused on the problems connected with big differences between techniques of production and, indeed, between the productivity functions themselves, corresponding to very great differences in the relative scarcity of factors of production and to immense differences in standards of living and the entire cultural setting.

Also, the theory of international trade more than any other branch of economic theory has been dominated by the assumption of stable equilibrium, implying the belief that normally a change will call forth as reaction secondary changes with an opposite direction. Only on this assumption—and, in addition, a number of other assumptions—does trade represent an element in the economic process which operates to bring about greater economic inequality between regions and countries.[7] Under the contrary and more realistic assumption, that more often the economic process is cumulative because of circular causation, the role of international trade becomes, as we have seen, rather the opposite one of being one of the media through which the market forces tend to result in increased inequalities when, as regularly in underdeveloped countries, the spread effects are weak.

[7] This criticism—in its negative form, that the equilibrium assumption and the theoretical approach which it represents are unrealistic—is, of course, anything but original, as I stressed in the last chapter. It has also often been pointed out that the theory of international trade, more than any other part of economic theory, has stubbornly remained an equilibrium theory. Professor John H. Williams, in his preoccupation with the relation between economic policy and theory, has observed as one of the greatest paradoxes of recent times that, "while since 1914 the world has been in a state of profound and virtually continuous disturbance, formal international trade theory has continued to emphasize equilibrating tendencies" (*Economic Stability in a Changing World*, Oxford University Press, 1953, p. 24); indeed "the main drift in theory, until recently at least, seems to have been toward further emphasizing equilibrating tendencies—whether through refinements on the classical analysis, or through the one of more modern value theory, or by introducing more countries and commodities. . . . The so-called 'modern' or Keynesian approach has carried this emphasis even further through its analysis of international trade adjustment in terms of income" (*ibid.*, p. 29).

There is another notion which joins with the equilibrium assumption in isolating the theory of international trade from the facts of international inequalities and the dynamic problems of under-development and development, namely, the distinction between "economic" factors and "noneconomic" ones. The noneconomic factors have much to do with what the classical economists referred to as "qualities" of the productive factors and, consequently, the "effectiveness" of production in various lines.

The classical economists cannot be accused of having overlooked the importance of the noneconomic factors. Indeed, Viner, to whom I have referred as the most prominent modern author in the great classical tradition, criticizes Heckscher and Ohlin for disregarding those aspects and continues:

> It is incumbent on the economist . . . to recognize and to proclaim that economic improvement is not merely a matter of more capital, or more acres, or more coal in the ground, but also of growth of effectiveness of management and of manual effort through better education, better health, better motivation, and better political and social organisation. If he fails to do so, he is liable to find himself throwing the blame for national poverty wholly on physical circumstances beyond human remedy, or on factors external to that economy, to the neglect of the internal human, social, political and moral factors which may carry a large part of the true responsibility.[8]

It is undoubtedly in this sphere of the "qualities" of the productive factors and, consequently, the "effectiveness" of production in various lines that a main part of the theoretical explanation has to be sought as to why countries have fared so unequally in their development and why international trade has not been active as an equalizing force. But lumping those things together under a single, abstract and vague concept and mostly dealing with this lump as a solid, static entity means precisely keeping them outside the analysis, i.e., abstaining from seeking the theoretical explanation demanded by establishing the interrelationships also with the noneconomic

[8] *Ibid.*, p. 16.

factors. And occasional references to individual elements within this lump and to their changes do not constitute a systematic explanation, linking economic development to economic theory, but represent rather a reversion to the indiscriminate "all case" method of the German historical school, which Viner least of all might be expected to find to his liking.

To define a certain set of phenomena as the "economic factors," while keeping other things outside the analysis, is a procedure closely related to the stable equilibrium approach. For it is precisely in the realm of those "noneconomic factors," which the theory of international trade usually takes as given and static, that the equilibrium assumption is most unrealistic and where, instead, circular causation is the rule.[9]

Effects on the Discussion of Underdevelopment and Development

The theory of international trade and its inherent ideological predilections have also had, of course, their influence—to some extent and more or less by implication—on the discussion in recent years of economic underdevelopment and development.

The facts of international economic inequalities and of their tendency to increase are awkward from the point of view of this theory, which had turned its back on these phenomena and even

[9] Already in his important paper from the late twenties, "The Theory of International Trade Reconsidered," Williams made the points that "the classical theory assumes as fixed, for purposes of the reasoning, the very things which . . . should be the chief objects of study if what we wish to know is the effects and causes of international trade, so broadly regarded that nothing of importance in the facts shall fail to find its place in the analysis"; and that "the relation of international trade to the development of new resources and productive forces is a more significant part of the exploration of the present status of nations, of incomes, prices, well-being, than is the cross-section value analysis of the classical economists, with its assumption of given quota of productive factors, already existent and employed" (*Economic Journal*, 1929, pp. 195 ff.). In the history of economics, Friedrich List has, of course, the honor of having early exposed the fallacy of assuming factor endowments as given. It is interesting to note that List exerted a great influence particularly in America—at the time when America was also an "underdeveloped" country, though in another sense as it had a very much higher level of income per head than those countries we now characterize as underdeveloped.

suggested that international trade had equalizing effects. This discord between facts and theory has not generally been stressed. Nor, in the discussion of underdevelopment and development, has there been much of a consistent attempt to pose as a main problem the explanation of the inequalities and their tendency to increase. Even today, when these facts are highlighted by the rising international political tension, there is very clearly an inclination to steer the discussion into other aspects of the problems of the underdeveloped countries than those related to international economic inequalities.

Similarly, this tendency inherent in the international trade theory has an interesting parallel in the type of discussion carried on in the developed countries about the commercial policies of underdeveloped countries. The advice most often given to the underdeveloped countries—that they should avoid tampering with trade and payments—and also the pressures exerted upon their commercial policies by means of the policies of the developed countries themselves are determined without much recognition of the dynamics of international economic inequalities.

Instead, most advice to the underdeveloped countries, and the pressures exerted upon them, are commonly rationalized in terms of a theory of international trade founded upon unrealistic assumptions so far as these countries are concerned. And the international organizations in the field of trade—the International Monetary Fund, the now-defunct International Trade Organization, and its remnant GATT—tend continuously to be permeated by the ideological elements which I have referred to as the predilections of economic theory and which have had a particularly strong influence on the theory of international trade.

The systematic bias which is at work in so many intellectual endeavors in connection with international policy prescriptions for the underdeveloped countries is related to the fact that the stable equilibrium approach is most often still the one predominantly used, and the further fact that the equilibrium concept is ideologically tied to the old and hardy predilections of harmony of interests, laissez faire and free trade. It is imbued wth a *telos* and objectified, and thereby hidden, valuations: it is seldom merely a theoretical tool chosen with full awareness of its complete arbitrariness from a policy point of view.

I observed in Chapter VIII that the paramount need for comprehensive state planning of economic development in underdeveloped countries is now generally recognized, not only in those countries themselves, but also by practically all economists and statesmen of the developed countries. Central economic planning and state interferences on a large scale to effectuate the planning are understood to be necessary as economic stagnation must be broken and as this will not happen if nothing is done to bring it about. But very apparently this recognition of a political necessity is in many quarters given very grudgingly and, when it comes to giving effect to this general policy of state interferences, all sorts of arguments to slip away into laissez faire raise their heads. This is particularly true in the field of international trade and payments where also the developed countries' interest in *status quo* is at stake.

The equilibrium approach, with its strong traditional ideological connotations, comes in then as convenient and opportune. For, while a realistic approach, recognizing the predominance in social developments of circular causation having cumulative effects, gives arguments for central planning of economic development in an underdeveloped country and large-scale state interferences, the equilibrium approach, because of the inherited ideological connotations, leads to laissez-faire conclusions.

When all this is said, however, it should be emphasized that on the whole the large and rapidly growing literature on the economic problems of the underdeveloped countries has paid little attention to economic theory generally or to the theory of international trade in particular. In its present stage this literature has on the whole a rather untheoretical slant. Indeed, at its best it seeks validity by keeping close to the ground of concrete facts and practical problems.

Most writers in this field express the desire for a theoretical framework. But this yearning is usually qualified by skepticism, sometimes amounting to total disbelief that we shall ever have a general theory of economic underdevelopment and development.

The Front against Iconoclasm

So far I have referred to the theory of international trade as if it were a single comprehensive system of thought which has to be rejected *in toto*, if the system is not accepted. Fortunately for my scientific conservatism, this is not the case. The system of thought I have criticized is actually a matrix of a large number of special theorems, most of which can be reshaped and fitted to other systems founded upon other assumptions.

This treasure of economic theorems has been steadily increased by the labor of many generations of theoreticians. Karl Menger once stressed that our science has been built up by scholars who mostly grudged themselves the leisure to reflect upon their own thinking and to question its logical foundations. And in the same spirit Knut Wicksell pointed out as the sign of a good economist that to a large extent he rises above the methods and assumptions he uses. On the basis of metaphysical notions and dominated by the opportunistic predilections, which I have attempted to characterize above, economists in every generation, beginning with the classical writers, have steadily increased our realistic knowledge about the world.

It was not my purpose on this occasion to expound this accumulated knowledge but rather to demonstrate and explain what I also believe to be true, namely, that the theory of international trade and, indeed, economic theory in general have never been developed to comprehend the reality of great and growing economic inequalities and of the dynamic processes of underdevelopment and development. And for this reluctance of economic theory to deal squarely with problems related to the equality issue there are explanations which should be spelled out if we want to free economic theory from its present inhibitions.

The fact that the theory now stands rather helpless when facing those problems does not mean that it cannot be successfully applied to other situations where there are no such great economic inequalities. Even the stable equilibrium concept, which, as I have argued, is unrealistic when used for studying normal social processes, might occasionally have a most useful role in the study of some problems, in particular when only a short period is under consideration.

And, as I said, most of the special theorems which make up the bricks of the big structure, the design of which I cannot accept, can with great advantage be utilized in quite another structure. Indeed, many of these theorems do not fit too well in the present structure but would fit excellently in the new one. The development of the "infant industry" argument and many other special considerations already taken account of by the classical economists, particularly as presented in their discussion of practical problems of the day, contained *in nuce* hints of a very much more realistic approach to the problems of the underdeveloped countries.

In recent decades much effort has also gone into connecting the developments in international trade with the cumulative processes analyzed in the framework of business cycle theory. Much of the discussion around the "dollar gap," as also concerning the importance for international trade and payments of demand and supply elasticities—sometimes leading to the notion of the possibility of "perpetual disequilibrium"—also has an unorthodox character.

If ever we come nearer to the formulation of a general theory of economic underdevelopment and development, it would remain a difficult but necessary task to integrate it into our general economic theory and, in particular, to make it and the theory of international trade consistent with each other. For, to hold logically unconnected and, in fact, mutually inconsistent theories is hardly a satisfactory state of affairs.

To accomplish this integration would most certainly, on the one hand, imply considerable adjustment and changes in general economic theory. The changes would then reflect the progress in our perception of the world economy attributable to the intensified studies of the long-term problems related to the facts of economic inequalities and the dynamic processes of underdevelopment and development.

On the other hand, the theory of underdevelopment and development, when once it is expounded, will not have been constructed simply out of a broad structural conception, like the one I have tried to sketch in Part One, plus empirical data: as building stones there will have been salvaged many familiar arguments and theorems now harbored in the broad framework of our general theories, including the theory of international trade, adjusted and fitted into the new structure. In economics, as in social theory generally, old thoughts are rarely discarded altogether, and no ideas are new and original.

The changed political situation in the world, the compulsion, implied in this changed political situation, to focus attention on entirely new and very different problems, and the appearance on the stage for the learned discourse of a host of new participants from nations which have until recently been kept passively submissive and mute are bound to represent the beginning of a revolution also in the social sciences, widening our horizon and radically redirecting our thinking. Out of this mighty process should also emerge a more realistic and relevant economic theory.

XII.

The Logical Crux of All Science

The Relation between the Moral and the Intellectual Discords

WHEN the facts of international economic inequalities and their tendency to grow are confronted with the state of public conscience in the richer nations and with the economic theory which has developed in the cultural setting of those countries, discords are brought into the open in both the moral and intellectual spheres.

Of these the moral discord is undoubtedly the fundamental one. On the one hand, there is in these nations, on the general plane of valuations, a common adherence to the ideal, inherited from far back in history, of the rights of all persons to equality of opportunity, independent of race and color, religion and creed, social status and nationality. On the other hand, in their daily life as individuals and as citizens, people there are not, in fact, prepared to take the consequences of this great moral principle, in a measure which even remotely approaches anything like completeness.

Economic theory is only a segment of the total culture. It becomes modulated to serve opportunistic rationalization needs. For people in these nations to live on as comfortably as possible with the moral discord in their hearts they need an economic theory directed in such a way that it turns attention as far as possible away from the moral discord.

This enhances the survival strength of those old doctrinal predilections of economic theory which have an instrumental value as antidotes to that theory's own basic equality doctrine, and also of such theoretical devices for "proving" those predilections as the stable equilibrium approach and the abstraction from the "non-economic" factors. The combined effect of these tendencies in economic theory—which are all logically related to each other and to the philosophies of natural right and utilitarianism from which economic theory has branched off—has been, and is, to keep theory aloof so far as possible from such facts and causal relations which, if analyzed, would focus attention on the economic inequalities as between regions and countries and thus on the fundamental moral discord.

In this situation the untheoretical twist which we have observed in the rapidly growing literature on the problems of the under-developed countries would seem to be a sound reaction on the part of the social scientists who are devoting their efforts to those problems. Attempting to do without a general theory would seem to be a safer course than using a biased and faulty one.

The Logical Necessity of a Theory and the Need of Adjusting It to Facts

It must be maintained, however, that theory is indispensable in scientific work. Theory is necessary not only to organize the findings of research so that they make sense but, more basically, to determine what questions are to be asked. Scientific knowledge never emerges by itself, so to speak, from empirical research in the raw, but only as solutions to problems raised; and such solutions presume a logically co-ordinated system of problems stated.

Theory, therefore, must always be *a priori* to the empirical observations of the facts. Facts come to mean something only as ascertained and organized in the frame of a theory. Indeed, facts have no existence as part of scientific knowledge outside such a frame. Questions must be asked before answers can be obtained and, in order to make sense, the questions must be part of a logically co-ordinated attempt to understand social reality as a whole. A non-theoretical approach is, in strict logic, unthinkable.

Underlying and steering every systematic attempt to find out the truth about society there is therefore always a theory: a broad vision of what the essential facts are and the causal relations between the facts. This theory which determines the direction of research should be made explicit. The danger of keeping the theory implicit—as unstated reasons for asking the particular questions that are asked and organizing the findings in the way they are actually organized—is, of course, that it escapes criticism.

If theory is thus *a priori,* it is, on the other hand, a first principle of science that the facts are sovereign. Theory is, in other words, never anything more than a hypothesis. When the observations of facts do not agree with theory, i.e., when they do not make sense in the frame of the theory utilized in carrying out the research, theory has to be discarded and replaced by another theory which promises a better fit.

Theory and fact-finding research should thus continuously be readjusted to each other, following the principle, however, that in the final analysis the facts are decisive. As the theory is merely a hypothesis, the criterion of its truth can never be anything else than the pragmatic one of its usefulness in bringing our observations of facts into a meaningful and noncontradictory system of knowledge. And so scientific progress can be expected to result by a process of trials and errors.

In the moral sphere, the corresponding logical process is moral criticism, proceeding on the assumption that there should be consistency between our valuations, a demand raised by feelings which are real because of the rationalism which is also part of our culture. As the valuations refer to social reality, and as therefore their interrelations logically involve people's beliefs concerning this reality, the process of correcting their theories to fit the facts has at the same time an important role to play in the attempts to give clarity, honesty and consistency to their moral ideas: to purify and strengthen the public conscience.

For people want to be rational. Scientific truth-seeking by rectifying the beliefs is also influencing the valuations. "In a rationalistic civilization it is not only that the beliefs are shaped by the valuations, but also that the valuations depend upon the beliefs." [1]

[1] *An American Dilemma,* p. xiv; cf. pp. 1028 ff.

The Provenance of Truthful Theory

For realism and relevance scientific research thus depends on a major *a priori*: an insight into what the essential facts and causal relations really are. This *a priori* theory then becomes corrected in the course of research to fit ever closer the reality studied. But from where, in the first place, is the *a priori* theory inferred? Where is its fountainhead?

To take it from one's own hunches is almost certain to be a choice of one of the innumerable roads to unreality and irrelevance. The theoretician's individual hunches do not even have the quality of being random, which would at least preserve a slight possibility that occasionally he would by pure chance strike upon what is essential and thus be in a position to pose questions which truly reveal reality and draw relevant inferences. For he is mostly, *nolens volens*, under the impact of the inherited theory which tends to serve as a vehicle for the predilections which I commented upon in Chapter X.

The "purer" a theoretician is the more he seems to be under the influence of the inherited predilections. The devotion of so much theoretical effort even in recent decades to "welfare economics"— though it was conclusively proved long ago that this approach is unrealistic and, in fact, without logical sense—is a demonstration of this point.

My next point is that there is no other rational way to reach that insight into what is really essential, and which is indispensable for the choice of variables for theory, than the cumbersome and laborious one of comprehensive and intensive empirical social science research. Only on the basis of a close contact with social history and social knowledge generally can we hope to construct the "model of the models" which could function as the guide to realism and relevance for our abstract theory.

This basic empirical research would need to encompass social facts and relations in all fields. In Chapter III I noted that our traditional division of knowledge into separate and delineated social science disciplines has no correspondence in reality: concrete problems are never simply economical, sociological, psychological or political. A theory of underdevelopment and development which works only with "economic" variables is for logical reasons doomed to be unrealistic and thus irrelevant.

And this comprehensive social science research prior to the construction of the abstract theory, and needed for assuring it realism and relevance, should be freed as far as possible from the powerful predilections I have referred to. The general method to accomplish this is to work with explicit value premises, themselves tested as to both relevance and significance.

This comprehensive research, however, needs itself, from the start and continuously as it proceeds, to formulate hypotheses in order to direct the observations and ask the pertinent questions. It needs theory. As I have just stated, empirical knowledge cannot be assembled and systematized without organizing principles, i.e., an insight into what are the essential facts and relations. Empirical research needs in fact for its own pursuit a nucleus of the theory which I am insisting can only be constructed on itself as a basis.

The Crux of All Science

This is the logical crux of all science: it assumes in all its endeavors an *a priori* but its ambitions must constantly be to find an empirical basis for this *a priori*. A worth-while theory of underdevelopment and development, if it ever could be formulated, would have to be based on ideas distilled from the broadest empirical knowledge of social change in all its manifold aspects, acquired under the greatest freedom from tradition-bound predilections. Only then can be safely founded the bold simplifications which can serve as the theoretical direction of research. But the empirical knowledge itself cannot be acquired without principles of selection and organization, i.e., without a vision of a theory.

We are thus constantly attempting what in its perfection is impossible and we are never reaching more than makeshifts: these, however, can be better or worse. In our present situation the task is not, as is sometimes assumed, the relatively easy one of filling "empty boxes" of theory with a content of empirical knowledge about reality. For our theoretical boxes are empty primarily because they are not built in such a way that they can hold reality. We need new theories which, however abstract, are more realistic in the sense that they are in a higher degree adequate to the facts.

Meanwhile, I believe it to be a disciplining force in our dispersed efforts in the field of underdevelopment and development that a clear concept of the ideal is constantly kept in mind and given a directing role in all our research. To begin with, we need to free ourselves from the impediment of biased and inadequate predilections and unreal and irrelevant theoretical approaches which in our academic tradition we are carrying with us as a heavy ballast.